Restored!

God's Salvage Plan for Broken Lives

Restored!

God's Salvage Plan for Broken Lives

Dan Schaeffer

DISCOVERY HOUSE
PUBLISHERS®

Discovery House Publishers is affiliated with RBC Ministries, Grand Rapids, Michigan.

Requests for permission to quote from this book should be directed to: Permissions Department, Discovery House Publishers, P.O. Box 3566, Grand Rapids, MI 49501, or contact us by e-mail at permissionsdept@dhp.org

All Scripture quotations, unless otherwise indicated, are from the NEW AMERICAN STANDARD BIBLE, updated edition. Copyright © 1960, 1962, 1963, 1968, 1971, 1972, 1973, 1975, 1977, 1995 by The Lockman Foundation. Used by permission. (www.Lockman.org)

Scripture quotations marked NIV are from the **HOLY BIBLE, NEW INTERNATIONAL VERSION®. NIV®.** Copyright © 1973, 1978, 1984 by Biblica, Inc. Used by permission of Zondervan. All rights reserved.

Interior design by Melissa Elenbaas

Library of Congress Cataloging-in-Publication Data

Schaeffer, Daniel, 1958-
Restored! / Dan Schaeffer.
    p. cm.
Includes bibliographical references.
1. Bible. O.T. Ruth—Criticism, interpretation, etc. I. Title.
BS1315.52.S36 2011
222'.3506--dc22

                                                        2010042765

ISBN 978-1-57293-454-2

Printed in the United States of America

Second printing in 2011

Contents

Is This Your Story?

DISTRESS: a painful situation: misfortune; a state of danger or desperate need

RESTORE: to put or bring back into existence or use; to put again in possession of something[1]

YEARS AGO A TEENAGE BOY LEFT HIS TEENAGE girlfriend and their young son. He never returned or stayed in contact with his son. The son grew attached to a new man, a second father, who married his mother. Then the man divorced his mother and forgot about the boy. A third father divorced his mother and only twice called the boy after the divorce, each time to try to get information about his mother.

The boy's life was in constant turmoil. Three "fathers" walked away from him as if he had never existed. His last name changed regularly, he moved frequently, and he witnessed constant tumult at home between his mother and each new man. Each experience, each change, seemed to make his life worse than it was before.

As a teenager, the son often wished he could put an end to his life, not wanting it to continue, not seeing any hope of positive change. When he was fourteen, his mother, overwhelmed by her own pain and suffering, attempted suicide and nearly succeeded.

The son felt that fate had given him a bad hand. Insecurities, fears, and doubts filled his life. He was a very distressed young man.

That young man is the author of this book.

I tell you this not to impress you with my difficulties, for many have faced far greater difficulties than I did, but to let you know that this book is not a dry treatise on distress and restoration. I have lived the truth of this book.

Have you lived a distressed life? Is this your story? Chances are good that you are experiencing distress and are desperate to find escape from it, hope within it, and especially restoration after it. Maybe you are in a fractured, stressful relationship or a troubled marriage. You may be in danger of losing everything due to the state of your finances. Maybe you have lost a loved one, your home, your job, or even the ability to work. Your children may be growing apart from you and dismissing everything you hold dear. Perhaps your health is declining. You are in "a painful situation . . . a state of danger or desperate need." You would like to know that it is all going to go away.

As a person who has recently passed the half-century mark, I can assure you that you have little chance of finding immediate escape from what is distressing you. And if you do escape distress, I can further assure you that it won't last. Distress is something we find ourselves wearing in this life, like clothes. The specific distress we are "wearing" this week may be different from the distress we were wearing last month, or last year, but distress is to this life what the four seasons are to earth—unchangeable, immutable.

As I said, I do not speak to you as a mere spectator on this subject but as a veteran campaigner. My younger years could best be described as "a painful situation . . . a state of danger or desperate need."

When I became a pastor I learned quickly that the life of a pastor is much like that of a police officer—the first person called to the scene of an accident. When calamity struck, or when broken relationships or circumstances were so overwhelming that they were no longer worth keeping secret, I was called in.

In short, I live and work in the continual shadow of distress in my own life and the lives of others. Yet, in spite of all the distress that I have endured in my life, I can honestly say with real and genuine conviction that while I would never want to go through what I endured again, I would not undo any of it.

Yes, you read that right.

The distress, as painful as it was, was the work of a Master Artist taking the pieces of a broken life and using them to create a mosaic of such beauty and wonder that it often brings me to tears of gratitude. I echo the heart and words of David in Psalm 16:5–6: "Lord, you have assigned to me my portion and my cup; you have made my lot secure. The boundary lines have fallen for me in pleasant places; surely I have a delightful inheritance" (NIV). I have experienced God's restoration—an amazing experience.

I remember the words of Joseph, so badly treated by his brothers and by circumstances; he was in one bad situation after another. After God delivered Joseph from his terrible circumstances, Joseph married and had two children. He named one son Manasseh, meaning "God has made me forget all my trouble and all my father's household," and the other Ephraim, because "God has made me fruitful in the land of my suffering" (Genesis 41:50–52 NIV). The Bible is littered with the accounts of His people in distress experiencing His restoration.

I do not expect you to be able to accept the idea of value in your distress—yet. I know that at this point you probably can't see any relief, restoration, or purpose for it all. Pain has a way of blurring perspective. But as we examine the restoration found in the pages of the tiny Old Testament book of Ruth, you will begin to see not only the hope of your restoration, but the need of it. When God restores us, He doesn't just take us back to where we were. He improves us, matures us, deepens us, and enables us to see the value the distress had in our lives.

This book is not another "trouble makes us stronger" bromide, because frankly, distress can also make us bitter, angry, resentful, fearful, and unable to enjoy our lives. I have experienced these emotions in response to my distress. Perhaps you are now struggling with some of these emotions. Your distress makes no sense to you and seems utterly bereft of any value. The truth is that those who respond favorably to the distress and those who respond tragically both endure the same emotions. Their experiences are similar, but their reactions differ. Why is this? Because we choose how we react to our distress. How we respond to our distress has much to do with the nature of our restoration.

When tyrants and dictators desire to punish their enemies, they work them to the point of physical exhaustion, driving them to endure more physically than they can stand. The punishment has but one purpose—to break down the individuals, to destroy their will to oppose the tyrant or fight back. The tyrant is frequently successful. The process leaves people weak and emaciated, skeletal ghosts.

When a football coach prepares his young athletes for the rigors of the season, he strengthens their bodies to be able to endure the physical abuse of the game. He exercises these young men to the point of physical exhaustion, pushing them almost more than they can stand. When he is done, these young men have been "distressed" into athletes whose bodies and minds and wills are stronger than they've ever been.

Both the tyrant and the coach "distress" their charges, but for dramatically different reasons. The victims of the tyrant chafe under the ill treatment but are forced to endure it. The young athletes also chafe under the treatment but accept it voluntarily and even gladly. The athletes see value in their distress. Athletes endure the physical pain and agony because they know conditioning makes them stronger, more agile, quicker, and better able to handle the physical beating of the game of football. The coach, though he has to pain and distress his young athletes, has only their best interests at heart. He would be a poor coach and a worse person if he neglected this aspect of their training and allowed them to be seriously hurt during a game.

In a world where people have abandoned belief in a sovereign and loving God who works His will mysteriously upon the earth, distress is seen as something to be avoided and escaped at all costs. Yet, distress is the necessary prelude to restoration. In the midst of our distress, God is at work to change the things we value, to help us see life from a different perspective. He is restoring us into His image and revealing himself to us in a deeper and clearer way.

In the pages of the Bible, we find a manual on restoration penned by the Holy Spirit. It is called Ruth, and it tells the story of two women who faced one distress after another with no hope for their situation to improve. It is a true story, so it contains what we would expect—initial despair and hopelessness about their situation. It also contains faith and courage, all from the same women. It is not the story of perfect women, but of human women responding to a level of distress that threatened to overwhelm them.

The main character in this powerful little book is never seen. He is the invisible God who works providentially behind the scenes, ever present and attentive, choreographing the movements in this gripping drama.

The story has one other essential character—and that is the person willing to take the amazing principles found in this story and apply them to his or her own distress. This is why God left us this precious book. That person is you. For in the book, we learn that restoration is real, life altering, and attainable by anyone who would submit himself or herself to the necessary process of restoration.

There is inestimable value in your current distress. It is far from random. It has a purpose and a goal and an objective far beyond anything you could imagine. It is no more designed to destroy you than is the surgery that removes the cancer, the shot that prevents the disease, the tourniquet that stops the hemorrhaging, or the first painful steps of therapy after reconstructive surgery.

A brilliant, divine picture, a portrait of you so beautiful you could never recognize it on this side of eternity, exists in the mind of our Lord, and each distress He allows in our lives is His divine brushstroke, adding color, maturity, depth of character, and a deep and eternal beauty that will be with you forever.

So journey with me as we view a divine snapshot in history, a moment that God etched forever on the pages of His eternal Word to remind us that distress, your distress, has great value, and that distress is but a prelude to the restoration God has planned.

The Story of Ruth

This brief synopsis of Ruth gives you an overview of the Old Testament book. I suggest reading the entire book of Ruth in your Bible.

During the period of the judges in Israel there was a famine. As a result, a man named Elimelech took his wife, Naomi, and two young sons, Mahlon and Chilion, to live in the land of Moab.

Tragically, Elimelech died in Moab, leaving Naomi a widow. Her two sons eventually married Moabite women named Orpah and Ruth. About ten years later, Mahlon and Chilion also died, leaving Naomi not only a widower, but bereft of her entire family as well.

Naomi heard that the Lord had blessed Israel with a great harvest and decided to return. Loyally and nobly, her daughters-in-law offered to return with her. But Naomi discouraged them, reminding them that they would be better off in Moab where their families could help them. She told them God was against her.

Anguished cries rose from their hearts as they clung to Naomi. Finally, however, Orpah returned to her household. Naomi urged Ruth to leave as well. Ruth refused, saying that no matter what happened to her, and no matter where Naomi went, she would go with her. Naomi's people would become her people, and Naomi's God would become her God. Naomi relented, and they traveled to Israel.

They arrived in Bethlehem, Naomi's hometown, at the time of the barley harvest. Ruth went to glean in the fields, a practice that allowed beggars to gather grain the harvesters missed. By God's providence Ruth happened upon the fields belonging to Boaz, a distant relative of Naomi's husband.

Boaz noticed the unfamiliar face among the gleaners and asked a servant about her. The servant informed Boaz that this young Moabite woman had returned with Naomi. Boaz kindly approached Ruth, encouraged her to glean in his fields where she would be protected, and commanded his servants not to bother her or stop her from gleaning. Ruth fell on her face in gratitude, confused as to why Boaz would be so kind to her, a foreigner—worse, a Moabite, for Israel and Moab were enemies. Boaz responded that he knew what she had done for her mother-in-law, and he approved of her decision to seek protection and provision from the God of Israel.

When it came time for a meal, Boaz invited her to eat with his workers, and when she rose to glean after the meal, Boaz commanded his reapers to purposely leave more grain behind for her to collect. So Ruth gleaned in the field until the evening, and then brought Naomi all she had collected. Out of curiosity, Naomi asked Ruth where she had gleaned. When Ruth told her about Boaz, Naomi remembered that Boaz was a kinsman redeemer. In Israel, a kinsman redeemer has the legal right to marry a deceased relative's wife to preserve the relative's name and memory in Israel.

Naomi encouraged Ruth to put on her best clothes and go to the threshing floor, where Boaz would be sleeping that night to protect his grain. Ruth was to uncover his feet and lie down, and then do whatever Boaz told her to do. Ruth did as her mother-in-law said.

In the middle of the night, Boaz woke up and realized that someone was sleeping at his feet. Boaz asked who it was, and Ruth answered him. She asked Boaz if he would be her kinsman redeemer. Boaz replied graciously, saying that she had shown kindness, for she could have sought a younger man to marry. Further, he said the women in the city had declared that she was a woman of excellence.

But Boaz informed Ruth that there was a closer relative who had a right to be the kinsman redeemer before him. He instructed Ruth to go back to sleep but to leave in the morning before anyone came to the threshing floor.

The next day Boaz found the nearer kinsman and called together the elders of the city. He told the nearer kinsman about Elimelech's land that Naomi needed to sell. He offered the land to the nearer kinsman. The nearer kinsman quickly agreed to redeem the land, but Boaz then informed him that he would have to marry Ruth the Moabitess and raise children to carry on the name of her dead husband and Naomi's dead husband.

The nearer kinsman balked and chose not to redeem the land, fearing that having children with Ruth would jeopardize his inheritance for his own children. Boaz declared before all those listening that he would buy the land of Naomi and marry Ruth to raise up children to her husband's name.

So Boaz married Ruth and cared for her and Naomi. Ruth gave birth to a boy and named him Obed. Naomi became Obed's nurse. Obed became the eventual father to Jesse, and Jesse became the father to David, the king of Israel.

CHAPTER 1

Ruth's Godly Character

*The great thing, if one can, is to stop regarding
all the unpleasant things as interruptions of one's
own or real life. The truth is of course that what
one calls the interruptions are precisely one's
real life—the life God is sending one day by day.
What one calls one's real life is a phantom of one's
own imagination.*

C. S. Lewis (1898–1963)

SEVERAL YEARS AGO, I WENT FISHING WITH SOME
men in the East Carson River around Lake Tahoe. We were fishing
for stream trout, mostly rainbow trout, trying our luck in different
spots on the stream. I found a small waterfall downstream that emptied into a perfect little pool. It was deep and a perfect spot for trout.

I threw my line into the pool and waited a few seconds until I
felt an inordinately strong bite. I was certain I had a large trout by
how hard it fought, but I wasn't able to see its size until the moment
I landed him on shore. Frankly, I was surprised and disappointed. It
was a decent pan size trout, but I was expecting a much larger fish
for the fight it put up. I put it on the line with my other trout and
since it was getting late, I headed back.

Soon the men brought their catches and laid them on the tailgate of the truck. I laid my fish on the tailgate with the others. Then one of our veteran fishermen said, "Hey, Dan, look at your fish! What a beauty! This is a *native*!" It's unusual to catch a native rainbow as nearby trout farms stock the streams. He motioned me to look at the difference between my fish and the other fish that had been caught. The difference was startling.

The native trout had brilliant, deep rainbow colors, especially compared with the dull color of the stocked rainbow. He also pointed out that the stocked rainbow's fins had been cropped, while the native rainbow's had not. The fish was drastically different in appearance from the others we had caught.

There are people like that "native" trout. They stand out from the crowd. They have the same appearance and speech as everyone else, but that's where the similarities end. They are an oasis in a desert, color in a world of black and white, originals in a world of reproductions—in short, godly. They do not seek conformity with the status quo. Such a person was Ruth.

DIFFICULT BEGINNINGS

The book of Ruth follows the book of Judges like the warm spring follows the frigid, dreary winter, thrusting forth beautiful flowers and verdant grass where before had been only deadness and cold. The story has a wholesome, clean, bright, and righteous tone that is so refreshing after the many failures of the nation of Israel. The period of the judges was a tumultuous, schizophrenic, and shameful time in Israel's history. In those days Israel had no king; they were a theocracy, which means they were ruled directly by God. Whenever the people wandered from worship of God or got themselves into difficulty, God would raise up human leaders, or judges, to turn their hearts back to Him and allow Him to bless them once again. However, after each judge died, the nation would return to its unfaithfulness.

This was the regular conduct of the people of God, the chosen people. At the end of this discouraging account of hit-and-miss faithfulness, of men and women doing "what was right in their own eyes" (see Judges 21:25), comes the story of Ruth—Ruth, who was not of the holy nation and chosen people, but was a lowly and destitute Moabite widow. Ruth did not grow up learning about God and worshiping Him. She had not received the law of God or the promises of Abraham. In fact, her ancestors had been a bur under the saddle of the nation of Israel. When the people of Israel had escaped bondage from Egypt and Moses was leading them through the wilderness, they had asked the people of Moab if they could walk through their land to shorten their journey. The people of Moab refused, and from that point on had caused problems for Israel. The nations warred constantly. Such was Ruth's heritage. She did not grow up loving and serving the God of Abraham, Isaac, and Jacob, but Chemosh, the detestable god of Moab.[1]

The book of Ruth is the story of how God takes a detested Moabite woman and makes her a woman of such unparalleled character and quality that even the Bethlehem Women's Club had to agree that she was a "woman of excellence." Ruth wasn't a likely candidate to have a book of Scripture written about her . . . or to become a great, great grandmother of King David, or even more important, a direct ancestor of our Lord Jesus Christ![2] The marvelous book of Ruth proves that the right heritage or background is not necessary to be greatly transformed and used by God. God calls the most unlikely people to be some of His greatest servants.

The book of Ruth demonstrates that even in a time of general moral and spiritual deterioration (such as the period of the judges), not everyone goes along with the crowd or checks to see which way the wind is blowing before deciding what he or she will do. Ruth especially was "a silver star in an inky sky, a glorious rose blooming amid desert aridness, a pure gem flashing amid foul debris, a breath of fragrance amid surrounding sterility."[3]

SHAPING

I once attended a pastor's conference where an artist demonstrated his unique skill. He was a sculptor . . . of a sort. His medium was wood—he used a common piece of tree trunk one might sit on, climb over, or burn in a fireplace. The artist stood in a soundproof booth with a large glass window in the front. You see, the artist sculpted with a chain saw. We watched as he cut, jabbed, and brushed the powerful and dangerous teeth of the chain saw against the log until a bald eagle slowly emerged. He spoke as he worked, effortlessly shaping the eagle while dispensing spiritual truths. If I hadn't seen it done myself, I would not have believed that such beautiful, delicate work could be done using such a dangerous and powerful tool. With one wrong move, the piece would have been ruined, the saw blade running through the wood like a hot knife through butter. Yet, within a few minutes, hundreds of pastors coveted the piece of art created before our eyes from a common log.

God did something in Ruth's life that He desires to duplicate in your life. He wants to make you into something uncommon and unnatural, unique and beautiful, but he doesn't begin with people who are unique and beautiful, *He makes them that way.*

We often bemoan the fact that we are not special, that we have no uncommon gifts, abilities, or talents. Like Ruth, who was a detested Moabite among Hebrews, we might be behind the talent and fortunate circumstance curve. We start the race knowing we're slower than everyone else, and sometimes we don't even get to begin until others are halfway around the track. Everything seems rigged against us. A sense of apathy and despair can seep into our hearts and minds. Yet it is in these circumstances that God creates godly people. He filled the pages of Scripture with stories about them so that we might learn that it is not our abilities or circumstances that matter.

Godly people start as common material, and common material has no value until the Master's skilled hands have formed it into something marvelous. That process involves something that we all would rather avoid: a strong and often painful shaping and molding.

Did you just wince? We shy away from this part. We prefer to keep our weaknesses, character imperfections, and sins firmly attached to us rather than endure the painful shaping by our Lord. The fact is that we don't often want to change—enough. Most of us would love nothing more than to be better people, to have a character much stronger than the one we currently have, to have a faith that would carry us into and out of even the darkest and bleakest situations. We'd just like these things to happen without any discomfort. We don't realize that the resistance to change is what makes us difficult to shape into better people with strong character and faith. Though we may detest our present situation, we still resist the necessary adjustments because, frankly, they hurt. We are often dragged kicking and screaming into the situation God will use to change us into His people. This is the case because we simply do not understand what He intends to shape us into or the difficult steps needed to create that beautiful character.

In the first chapter of Ruth, we learn that Ruth has to leave her country, family, and religion to accompany her beloved mother-in-law and follow her new God. In the second chapter of Ruth, we see that Ruth, while willing to leave her comfort zone, was struggling with the process. She had been jerked out of everything familiar and thrust into a different country and lifestyle. Her life wasn't easy or fun, and nothing on the horizon made it look like that was ever going to change.

In hindsight we see the necessity of Ruth's choice to leave and the wonderful hand of God in all of it. But do you think she saw the situation then as clearly as we see it now? The story makes it clear she didn't. How could she? She didn't understand the purpose of her distresses any more than we understand ours.

Countless people have left their countries, homes, and even families because a future in a strange and unfamiliar America looked better to them than staying where they were. But that's what makes Ruth unique: there was nothing better waiting for her where she was going. She was walking into the unknown with the conviction that where she was going would be worse for her than where she was leaving. She wasn't escaping a bad situation to enter a better one. That would make perfect sense. She was doing the opposite, and that only makes sense through the eyes of faith.

Yet I believe that she didn't falter for a moment, because while she would be leaving security and comfort behind in Moab, she knew that there was only one true God, and He was Jehovah, and she had become His servant. She no longer valued anything in Moab. Naomi, her devout Hebrew mother-in-law, was dearer to her now than her real family because she and Ruth shared the same faith.

Had Ruth insisted on having a convenient life, holding on to her heritage, her religion, her family, and her old way of life, the story of Ruth would never have been told, because there never would have been a story worth telling. Some things in our lives require removal to guarantee our continued growth. That removal is painful and scary but absolutely necessary.

Unfortunately two opposing desires pull us in two different directions. These desires are not abnormal, nor a sign of God's displeasure in our lives. One desire is to change and become everything God wants us to be. The other desire is to resist that change because we realize it will be initially painful or difficult. The result is that we remain too paralyzed to make a move, so God, in His mercy, intervenes. Often God's shaping of our lives will involve discomfort, fear, loss, reversal, and movement away from the familiar and secure, but this movement is not a punishment—it is a prescription. I challenge you to find someone who has a wonderful and amazing character who has not gone through great difficulty and pain.

At this point many of us, if we could, would ask for a time-out to reevaluate our participation in this process. We're not sure we really want to go through a painful shaping. But that's not the whole story . . . it gets worse before it gets better. When we go through difficult times, we are as likely to learn the wrong lesson as the right one. I know that from experience. To ensure the beautiful creation God has made in our lives remains, another step must be taken, the step that will finalize and make our new condition permanent: firing in the furnace.

FIRING IN THE FURNACE

You probably don't like the sound of this step any more than I do, yet it is essential! Being able to withstand the searing heat of trials is part of becoming godly. After an artisan has molded and shaped his or her vase or statue, the artist fires it in a furnace at a high temperature to solidify it. You see, while the piece has the shape the artist desires, the material is still too soft, pliable, and vulnerable. The work can easily become misshapen or deformed by the slightest amount of pressure. To keep the creation the way He designed it, God applies the heat of distress, which serves to harden it. This hardening is designed to strengthen, not shatter, the design. The process makes the creation's beauty permanent.

What does the process of firing look like in our lives? Firing occurs when negative circumstances challenge the new value or character that God has recently (or not so recently) shaped in us. While we can make a decision to change and approach life with a new perspective (New Year's resolutions, good intentions, etc.), we have not made that change permanent by acting on it during distress. God wishes to solidify our decision to change by having us act in a way that makes clear that we really are different than we were before. If we choose to jettison our new values and behavior because they will cost us, then we have not truly owned the changes we had implemented. If, on the other hand, we, like Ruth, choose the new course in spite of opposition or negative circumstances, then we have been hardened by God's firing process. Our new character has withstood the test of trials, and we have been "petrified" into a new godly form or attitude.

When Ruth makes that beautiful commitment to Naomi to follow her into her country, leaving all she had behind, she is being shaped by God. When she arrives in the land of Israel, God fires her in His furnace. Instead of being comfortable in her new country, she is reduced to begging for her life. Gleaning, which was Israel's form of welfare, instituted by God, was the only way she and Naomi could stay alive. Gleaning was the process where the poor could follow the farmhands who harvested the wheat or grain, and whatever the farmhands didn't collect, they could pick up. While this was a great system, not all farmers were godly men. Some would instruct their workers to beat the gleaners who came too close to their crops. Gleaning in the fields could be risky and dangerous. This was what Ruth had to endure in the land of Israel—living on the tenuous kindness of others.

The process of becoming godly requires being fired in the furnace. You cannot bypass this process if you desire to become God's original, unique creation. I won't pretend that you can't find ways to escape problems if you are willing to compromise, ignore God's will, or concern yourself only with your own comfort and convenience— but the escape will be temporary. When trouble returns, as it will, you will be vulnerable, unprepared, and lacking the wisdom and character to make godly, safe, and correct decisions.

I have watched dozens of Christians try to escape distress in their lives and the results were always tragic. We need firing in the furnace or we become crippled, like the butterfly that is pulled from its cocoon. The butterfly's struggle to push its way through the tiny opening of the cocoon pushes the fluid out of its body and into its wings. Without the struggle, the butterfly would never fly. Sadly, withdrawing from the necessary step of being fired in the furnace keeps you from reaching the result of the process, the goal we all covet: becoming what you really want to be, a unique creation of value and worth—godly. If you only see the process and don't look at the goal of the finished product, you will resist the shaping or try to escape the fire designed to strengthen God's working in your life.

You may look at your life now and not see a godly person in progress. Sometimes you probably feel more like a play dough creation, something squeezed through a small plastic tube and coming out looking much like a mutant snake. The hard reality is that our best moments often follow our worst. If you search the pages of Scripture, you will see that our greatest heroes before their great moments were at their weakest, when things looked the bleakest, when it made the most sense to abandon faithfulness and obedience. But it was in those moments that they stayed the course. The next step was often their deliverance.

The distress we endure serves to illustrate what kind of people we are becoming. In other words, the distress God brings into our lives doesn't just shape us, it reveals the shaping (or lack of it) that has already been done. Distress in Ruth's life revealed her solid character. Distress in Naomi's life revealed some character blemishes that God wanted to shape away. Later we see that the process of shaping and firing left Naomi unselfish and able to focus on her daughter-in-law's opportunities.

It's easy to discount this shaping and firing process by saying that God couldn't make anything special out of me because I'm not anything special to begin with, or that distress has revealed me to be lacking. That assumes that God needs special, perfect material to make His original creations. He doesn't! He never has. Let's not forget that He created Adam and Eve out of common dirt! It's the skill of the Maker and Designer, the Master Artist, that is at issue. Are you willing to say that God isn't powerful enough to make something incredible out of you?

If you are a child of God, I have an important message for you. The God of all creation, the One who spoke all things into existence, the source of all beauty and power and wisdom, is planning on making a godly person out of you. Part of that process involves distress. You can either cooperate in the process, or resist it. Frankly, those are your only two options.

Imagine what Ruth would have become had she chosen to chart the easy course in life. No one can really know—but it's a safe bet we would have never heard of her. Ruth's distress—the loss of her husband, the challenge to accept a new faith in a new God, the difficulty of leaving her family and country—has helped to shape the godliness we see in her. The firing of leaving her home and journeying to a foreign land, knowing the difficulties she would encounter there, revealed that the change had become permanent. She would not go back on her decision or her commitments.

Her distresses not only formed her into a godly person, they revealed her to the world as one. The same awaits you.

The same choices.

The same opportunities.

BECOMING GODLY

Distress revealed that Ruth had cultivated a set of amazing character qualities that God used to lead her providentially in her restoration. A wonderful hope we have is that as we cultivate such character qualities, God will use them to bring the deliverance we so desperately need. Ruth's time had not been wasted as she developed her character.

We choose what characteristics we want to adopt into our own lives. This is a truth that our world forgets. We are told that our background and experiences conspire to shape who we are and how we act. But while those things can *affect* us, they don't *determine* us. We are shaped by our *choices*. We can't choose our personalities or temperaments, and we can't choose the environment we grew up in or some of the experiences we've had to endure, but we can choose what we will cultivate in our lives.

Over time we develop patterns of behavior as we make the same choices over and over. Sometimes it takes years for these patterns to develop, but they eventually become our modus operandi for every situation. We begin to approach every problem and situation the same way. Ruth did too, and because of the choices she made and the patterns she developed, she is an example of that rare quality we can only describe as godly. Let's look at Ruth and see if we can discover the elements of a godly character.

Selflessness

Naomi tries to talk Ruth out of following her. Naomi reminds Ruth that if she follows her she can expect no husband, no children, and no material security. That's what following God and Naomi would cost Ruth. The only guarantee she had was that she would be a no one, associated with a nobody, who together had nothing! At this point any false humility would have melted away quickly. But Ruth was the picture of selflessness. It had become instinctual for her to think of others as more important than herself. She ignores her dismal situation to take care of Naomi. She then marries an older man, Boaz, when Boaz admits that she could have married a rich young man.

She's the proverbial doormat, giving up her life for someone else. Can you imagine how she would have been chided by today's advice givers?

"Your responsibility is over Ruth; it's time to live for yourself."

"You take care of *yourself*—let Naomi take care of *herself*."

"You're crazy. You'll be losing everything you've gained in life."

"Let her family take care of her, Ruth."

Ruth didn't appear to find her chosen lifestyle offensive. Naomi tries to talk her out of it but can't! From Ruth's perspective, she was getting ahead in everything that mattered to her.

Maybe, just maybe, Ruth discovered something we have missed. Ruth had come to understand, through experience, that there is a joy in serving others, and it is more blessed to give than to receive, and humility does come before honor. Distress strips away the false pretension we build up. Ruth's distress enabled her to not only act humbly, but to think humbly. Her selflessness was genuine.

Trust

Ruth trusted that the God of Israel would protect and deliver her, and she put her life on the line to prove it. She exhibited trust in the cold, dreary winter of her life. She believed that God would help her, but she had no idea what that help would look like or when it would come. Her faith was in things hoped for and things not yet seen, because her faith was in God's work on her behalf in a future that she had yet to experience.

In a beautiful passage, Boaz says to Ruth, "May the Lord reward your work, and your wages be full from the Lord, the God of Israel, under whose wings you have come to seek refuge" (Ruth 2:12). Boaz clearly saw her trust, and admired and praised it. Her trust in God was obvious to all.

To trust God when everything is positive, safe, and secure is not difficult. To trust God that He will deliver you, will provide for you, will help you when no external signs confirm that fact is the hardest thing in the world to do. Distress is a wonderful tool for removing the "props" that we often rest our faith upon. When it seems as if God has abandoned us, He has not; He has just given us the opportunity to exercise our flabby muscles of faith.

Kindness

When Ruth makes her famous and beautiful confession to Naomi, who was trying to convince her to go home to her family in Moab where better things would await her, Naomi and Ruth were the only ones there. Orpah, Naomi's other daughter-in-law, had already gone. There was no audience to impress. Let's read these precious words from a daughter-in-law to her mother-in-law:

> Do not urge me to leave you or turn back from following you; for where you go, I will go, and where you lodge, I will lodge. Your people shall be my people, and your God, my God. Where you die, I will die, and there I will be buried. Thus may the Lord do to me, and worse, if anything but death parts you and me. (Ruth 1:16–17)

This is kindness in a lonely place. Ruth didn't simply say I won't leave you, but that she was joining herself to Naomi's welfare. Whatever befell Naomi would befall Ruth. Wherever Naomi went, and whatever she encountered, good or bad, was what Ruth was signing up for. No exceptions, no small print at the bottom of the contract.

True kindness is unexpected, humbling, and so rare that few can say that they have seen it. It's rarer than a snow leopard, an honest politician, or winning the lottery, and it can't be faked. The reason it is so rare is because it has to spring from something equally rare—a heart that has ceased to think about itself and its own needs and instead has focused on someone else's needs.

Distress was the black light that revealed the true kindness that existed in Ruth. It had been planted and nurtured in Ruth's heart, but distress brought it to light and revealed its growth. What was true in Ruth's life is true in ours as well. Distress is often the thing that exposes character.

DO YOU REALLY WANT TO BE DIFFERENT?

I have never met anyone who told me that his only goal in life was to be just like everybody else. Most people I know desperately want to be different, in a positive way. If you told someone that she was a reproduction, just like everyone else, she would be offended.

God wants to make you something very, very special. He wants you to stick out in this world like a beautiful rainbow trout, because that's what He's in the business of doing. But you have to let Him do the whole process, not run away in the middle of distress, not quit in the middle of a struggle.

Restoration, complete restoration of your heart and mind, begins not with your circumstances, but your choices. Circumstances are out of your control—not so choices.

To become godly involves allowing God to remove all those things in our lives that mar the beauty He intends to create in us. I won't lie—it's not easy, as we will see in the next chapter with Naomi. But keep in mind an important truth: the distress that God brings into our lives has far more benefits than drawbacks.

CHAPTER 2

Naomi's Character Blemishes

Many men owe the grandeur of their lives to their
tremendous difficulties.

Charles Haddon Spurgeon (1834–1892)

MANY YEARS AGO A FRIEND OF MINE SHOWED ME
how to restore old wooden furniture. After his lesson, I was eager
to begin. I had two problems getting started: I didn't have pieces to
work on or money to buy them. While attending a neighbor's garage
sale, I spied an old half-circle wooden table that had sat on the porch
for years. The family had used it to hold junk, and it had numer-
ous deep, black circles of water stains. The years of neglect and the
ravages of weather had removed all vestige of its original condition.
What attracted me to the sad piece of neglected furniture was that
it was wood.

My neighbor sold me the table for three dollars. The way I
looked at it, I had nothing to lose because the piece couldn't look any
worse if everything went wrong. More importantly, I could practice
what I had learned without risking a costly mistake.

So, I began. I started sanding . . . and sanding . . . and sanding.
The table's wooden legs were so wobbly that they could no longer
support the tabletop, and I wondered if I could ever get it to stand
by itself. I looked at the legs, realized that they were fixable, and

set about repairing them. And then I sanded again. The dark stains were so deep that it took hours of hand sanding to reach that layer of untarnished wood.

Finally I had the piece sanded and the legs repaired. It was difficult to tell what kind of wood it was, and I was pondering what kind of stain I should apply when I accidently dripped water on the dry wood. As I reached to wipe it away, I froze. The water revealed an incredibly beautiful, dark, and luxurious wood. Excited now, I applied a lacquer finish to the wood, and the onetime piece of junk became a brilliant piece of furniture once again. That table now sits proudly in our living room, a reminder that restoration is an amazing process, and that the effort is well worth the result.

Nothing survives the rigors of time and life without some wear and distress. Dumps and junkyards are filled with once valuable items that have been distressed by life's pressures and tossed out. Some of us who have gone through terrible distress often feel like we are ready for the human junkyard and that any value we once had has vanished. But in the same way that the process of distress and restoration adds character, value, and beauty to physical things, so it also is God's way of adding these same things to our lives.

We've discussed how distress can show off a godly character, but sometimes distress reveals stains that need sanding or rough edges that the Master Sculptor needs to chip away. Distress is His tool to both reveal and to shape. So, as counterintuitive as it may sound, there are times in our lives when God causes us to be distressed. He authors it for the very purpose of conforming us into the image of His beloved Son. Sometimes our own sinfulness and mistakes create the distress in our lives, but not always! Some distress we encounter, the pain we experience, is not related to any sin on our part, but is God's way of adding depth and maturity to our lives. Most of us would love to go through life without any dings, wear, or tear, but were we to get such a life, we would not gain the depth, maturity, and grace God's work in our lives produces.

Distress and restoration is a process we would just as soon bypass, but the distresses of life are necessary: they are the strokes of a Master Artist, who is making His children look more and more like Him—from the inside out.

In this chapter we are going to look closer at the life of Naomi, Ruth's mother-in-law, for her life holds some tremendous lessons for us. Initial distress revealed three things in Naomi's life that God wanted to shape away: she desired isolation, failed to trust God, and forgot her purpose. God wanted better for Naomi. Remember, God is not restoring us to the place we were in before, or to the type of person we were before, but to a better place and a better person. He is restoring us into His image. We see in the book of Ruth distress born of God's purpose to add to Naomi's life something that could not be added any other way.

NAOMI DESIRED ISOLATION

For years Naomi had what every Hebrew woman wanted, a husband for security and sons for posterity. She was a woman every Jewish woman would consider greatly blessed. Then she went from a position of strength and honor, with a husband and two sons, to a position of weakness and shame when her husband and sons were taken from her. She is left alone in Moab with her two daughters-in-law and a crushing despair. In her pain and despondency, she tells both her daughters-in-law, Orpah and Ruth, that they should go back to their own families for she has nothing to offer them. Hope had died inside of Naomi, and she tells her daughters-in-law to leave her. As Norman Cousins wrote, "Death is not the greatest loss in life. The greatest loss is what dies inside of us while we live."[1]

When we are not in great pain or distress, we often keep people around us at a distance. If your arm feels fine, why have doctors or nurses poking around to see where a future break might occur? Where there is no perceived need, there is rarely a sense of vulnerability, and therefore little opportunity for others to speak to us, console us, comfort us, provide for us, and listen to us. It is the arrival of distress that changes our minds.

People whose lives are going swimmingly tend to find it difficult being vulnerable and struggle accepting help. They want to be helpers, but they don't always welcome help themselves. They pride themselves on their resources and independence. They erect great fortresses around their lives with a moat and guards at every parapet. These people are friendly enough at a distance, but no one, absolutely no one, gets in the fortress. They do this hoping to remain safely insulated from pain—but nothing in this life can do that. Nothing. All they manage to do is insulate themselves from the wonderful relational anesthetic God has created for the deepest pain—the demonstrative love of those who care deeply about us.

We see that Naomi was able, in the midst of her distress, to send Orpah away, and probably to believe that Ruth would follow her. It was a noble and valiant effort, trying to see to the needs of others she cared about, but it also revealed her strong and independent nature. It would behoove us to remember that in sending away her daughters-in-law, Naomi was effectively removing all companionship.

Naomi would return home alone. This wasn't a two-hour drive in the family station wagon, but depending on where they settled in Moab, the trip would be seventy to a hundred miles and would take about a week. On foot! She would return home childless. She would return home destitute. She would return home hopeless! And this is probably the most distressing thing there is in life, to lose your hope!

Naomi was determined to "go it alone." How many people today are trying to do that? Are you? Surrounded by people who want to help and encourage you, are you insisting on going it alone? Maybe that's what you've been doing all your life. It may sound brave and spiritual, but it runs counter to the entire New Testament that reveals that we are meant to be in close relationship with other believers. There is no island in the church of Jesus Christ! We are to "rejoice with those who rejoice, and weep with those who weep" (Romans 12:15). It may be humbling to hear that God designed you to need others, but it is true, and when that truth is accepted, it is one of the more freeing truths in life.

In Ruth 1:8–15 we read that Naomi tried to talk Ruth into leaving, but when Ruth resisted, Naomi finally broke down. She allowed Ruth to be her friend, her companion, her child, her hope. *That's precisely why God had provided Naomi with Ruth.* Only distress could have broken Naomi's tight grip on "going it alone." I have noticed that distress makes people willing to allow others to minister to them at a deeper level than ever before. Only distress makes them take that chance at vulnerability.

Naomi's distress was what opened that door. Both Orpah and Ruth were companions in Naomi's success, but now Ruth was not only willing (as was Orpah), but *insistent* on being a companion in Naomi's distress! In hard times, we discover what we may have overlooked in times of joy.

In 1999 a painting that had hung unnoticed for nearly seventy years in a dark corridor of a Jesuit center in Pennsylvania was discovered to be a rare and valuable work by Tintoretto, a sixteenth-century Venetian artist. The painting, *The Raising of Lazarus,* was estimated to be worth as much as two million dollars. The Jesuits had always thought it to be a reproduction. The couple who had donated it had paid thirty-five thousand dollars for the work in 1928. The Reverend J. A. Panuska, rector of the Jesuit Novitiate Spiritual Center in Lower Heidelberg Township in Pennsylvania, said, "Nobody really paid much attention to it. It was overlooked. We just sort of hung it."[2] What was overlooked was not the painting; it had been in constant sight for many years. What was overlooked was its true value. It wasn't until an expert passed by and noticed it that its value was realized and people began to appreciate it for what it was.

Certain people in our lives are like that painting. We notice them and appreciate their friendship, but we have no idea their true value until we find ourselves in deep distress. That distress will be the catalyst to reveal a depth of loyalty and love we never knew existed. True distress distills our acquaintances, separating the gold from the dross, the casual friends from those precious few who will refuse to leave us and will insist on walking with us through our trouble. Distress allows others to love us in ways they never could before—revealing to us the love we had never known existed.

Let's read again Ruth's beautiful words to Naomi:

> Do not urge me to leave you or turn back from following you; for where you go, I will go, and where you lodge, I will lodge. Your people shall be my people, and your God, my God. Where you die, I will die, and there I will be buried. Thus may the Lord do to me, and worse, if anything but death parts you and me. (Ruth 1:16–17)

Ruth, in this beautiful confession, reveals the depth of commitment and love she had for Naomi. The words would have seemed awkward or out of place without the deep distress in Naomi's life.

How comforting it must have been to Naomi to know that after all she had been through, she wouldn't have to walk alone, and she wouldn't have to hurt alone. Naomi needed the deep commitment and love that Ruth offered her at that desperate point in her life. Don't you see that nothing less would have met her need, *and God knew it?* He knew it before Naomi knew it. How intimately He knows us!

Ruth's amazing and memorable words of love and loyalty would never have been uttered were it not for Naomi's distress. Think about that. Some of the most famous words in the Bible were prompted by a distress so deep and painful that no other words, no lesser exclamation would do. The feelings were always there—the depth of love was always there—but deep distress was the only catalyst that could draw them forth.

There are people around us now who are more committed to us than we could ever imagine, and we won't really find out who they are until we encounter distress. Proverbs 20:6 reminds us that "Many a man proclaims his own loyalty, but who can find a trustworthy man?" We often discover that trustworthy man or woman when distress arrives, seldom before.

Who has God put into your life to help you in your distress? Are you reaching out to them, or are you rebuffing them? Is there a caring, godly person who God might want to use to minister to you at a deeper level than ever before? Be careful that you are not pushing away the very means of restoration and hope God is sending your way.

NAOMI FAILED TO TRUST GOD

We treat God much the same as we treat everyone else. If we are willing to allow people access to us in times of distress, we will allow God access to us in those times. However, if we aren't willing to allow people access to us in time of need, we aren't likely to allow God access to us either.

As we limit others' ministry to us, so we limit God's ministry to us—*for a large part of His ministry comes through those He has sent our way.* Naomi would have needed to trust God before her time of great distress, but it seems evident that she never had to trust God for her very life, livelihood, and emotional stability in a time of catastrophe. She had her husband before, and two sons, and two daughters-in-law.

Trusting God when nothing is at stake is easy. In hard times, God is asking the question, Can you trust me *now*?

- You could trust me when you had a spouse, but can you trust me now?

- You could trust me when you had a job, but can you trust me now?

- You could trust me when you had your health, but can you trust me now?

- You could trust me when you had money in the bank, but can you trust me now?

- You could trust me when you first got married, but can you trust me now?

- You could trust me when everything was going well, but can you trust me now?

Can you trust me now?

One thing I have learned is that "negative" circumstances don't always turn out badly, and "positive" circumstances don't always turn out well. We just don't know what circumstances mean when they arrive. Losing a job can seem like a negative circumstance until you get a better job than you had before. Getting a great new job with high pay can seem like a positive circumstance until you realize the work environment is detrimental to your mental and emotional health. For Naomi, everything looked negative, bleak, and hopeless, yet her deliverance was right at hand. God needed to teach her that she could trust Him *even now*.

We don't have to guess at Naomi's feelings during her ordeal, as they are revealed to us when she finally returns to Bethlehem and is greeted by the local women:

> So they both went until they came to Bethlehem. And when they had come to Bethlehem, all the city was stirred because of them, and the women said, "Is this Naomi?" She said to them, "Do not call me Naomi; call me Mara, for the Almighty has dealt very bitterly with me. I went out full, but the LORD has brought me back empty. Why do you call me Naomi, since the LORD has witnessed against me and the Almighty has afflicted me?" (Ruth 1:19–21)

As Naomi reentered her hometown after ten years away, some of the women were saying, "Is this Naomi?" When we read Naomi's rather bitter response, we can be confused by it until we learn that Naomi's name meant "pleasant." We can more fully understand the source of Naomi's pain when we realize that in her deep despair, she heard her old friends saying, "Is this the pleasant one?" That must have felt like a blow to an open and tender wound. Her natural human response is, "No, I'm not pleasant, I'm bitter. I went out pleasant, but I came back bitter."

There are times in life when we can't see around the corner, we can't guess what is going to happen with our circumstances, and everything looks bleak and hopeless. Like Naomi, we have to ask ourselves the question, Can I trust Him *even now?*

God wanted Naomi to know that He was more than a spectator God. He wanted her to know that He was intimately acquainted with and intimately involved with her life and that He could minister to her and comfort her in deeper tragedies than she had ever known. In short, He wanted to show Naomi that she could trust

Him even now. Often we struggle with the same thing—we don't really believe that God can create anything good out of our horrible situations. The example of Naomi shows that distress is the very thing that God often uses to prove to us that we can trust Him even when circumstances look bleak.

NAOMI FORGOT HER PURPOSE

It is often easy to forget what our real purpose is before God when we are busy trying to make our lives comfortable, profitable, and enjoyable. The church creeds make it clear that now, as always, our purpose on this earth is to glorify God. It was our Lord's first and greatest purpose, to glorify His Father in heaven. Is it still ours?

Was it ever?

When we enter the last chapter of Ruth, we find a different Naomi than the one we started with. In the first chapter, distress had revealed that Naomi forgot her purpose to glorify God regardless of the circumstances. In the last chapter of Ruth, we witness Naomi's great transformation and blessings, the result of her and Ruth's ability to trust God even through terrible distress. She has rediscovered her purpose. While God did allow her to lose a husband and two sons, He provided Ruth, and through Ruth another son, and this son would be an ancestor to King David and ultimately to Jesus Christ.

Naomi, as a faithful Hebrew, could not have imagined a higher honor or greater blessing than to be included in the genealogy of her Messiah. God wasn't just blessing Naomi in the present life, which she could easily experience, but He was going way beyond that blessing to put her smack-dab in the middle of the line of Christ. She would be blessed for millennia to come. Even today Naomi is being blessed and her God is being glorified. The plans of God that we are allowed to witness go far beyond the present in our lives, and His blessings to us and our progeny can, like Ruth and Naomi, be sent into the future. Though Naomi resisted her distress because she did not understand its purpose, God has been abundantly glorified through Naomi and her experiences. She never knew about it, but we do, because we can look back. There are times when our pain and distress are designed to bring glory to God, period! Our reaction to distress is to be a witness to how God can meet the deepest needs of people. As others see God meet our needs, His faithful provision often draws them to Him. His people never travel any road alone—He is always there, even when He can't easily be seen.

Paul in 2 Corinthians 12:7–10 tells of a "distress" that God brought into his life. He called it his "thorn in the flesh." It was probably a physical affliction that constantly hounded him. Paul says he asked God three times to please remove it, but God said no. Then God gently reminded the great apostle that "My grace is sufficient for you, for power is perfected in weakness."

Many of us have sung the words, "In my life, Lord, be glorified, be glorified today."[3] We sing this song as a prayer to God, often unaware of its implications. Then God faithfully answers our prayer and begins to glorify himself in our life through distress or pain, and we yell, "Stop! Stop being glorified in my life, Lord. Be glorified in *someone else's life*." And He gently answers, "No. My grace is sufficient for you, for my power will be perfected in your weakness."

One day Jesus was walking by a lame man, prompting His disciples to ask a question that highlighted the thinking of their day. His answer is enlightening.

> As He passed by, He saw a man blind from birth.
> And His disciples asked Him, "Rabbi, who sinned,
> this man or his parents, that he would be born
> blind?" Jesus answered, "It was neither that this man

sinned, nor his parents; but it was so that the works
of God might be displayed in him." (John 9:1–3)

The pressing question was who committed the sin that led to this
man's terrible distress, and Jesus' answer was "neither." This distress
was so that God may be glorified, that in a marvelous way His works
would be displayed through the lame man's life. Some distress is for the
purpose of glorifying God and is not connected to any particular sin.

The ultimate goal of humankind is to glorify God. No Christian would deny that, but many would deny Him the opportunity
in their own lives if they could. I know there are times that I would
have. But the end result, after God meets you in that special way, is
that not only is God glorified through it, but you are stronger and
more mature because of it and glad it happened because of the effect
it had on you. A. B. Simpson wrote,

> If we would be enlarged we must accept all that
> God sends us as His own divinely appointed
> means of developing and expanding our spiritual
> life. We are so content to abide on the old plane
> that God has often to compel us to rise to a higher
> level by bringing us face to face with situations
> which we cannot meet without greatly enlarged
> measures of His grace. To use a suggestive figure,
> He has to send the tidal wave to flood the lowlands
> where we dwell that we may be compelled to move
> to the hills beyond; or, to take a more scriptural
> and beautiful figure, like the mother bird, He has
> to break up our downy nest and to hurl us into
> empty space, where we must either learn to use an
> entirely new and higher method of support or sink
> into destruction.[4]

WHAT WILL DISTRESS REVEAL IN YOU?

There is real value in distress, even though distress is not pleasant at the time. God, through our distress, reveals to us the person we are becoming and shapes us into a person more like His Son. As you face your distress today, maybe your greatest need is to gain perspective on it. Circumstances can look so negative at times, and yet we see through Naomi's life that we don't know what circumstances mean, so we must be careful not to get too discouraged by them. Circumstances that look terrible and bleak (like losing a husband and two sons) don't mean you will never find joy and happiness again. They don't mean that God does not still have a wonderful purpose for your life. Naomi couldn't possibly have known what her circumstances meant at the time; neither can we know what our circumstances mean at present.

What we can know is this: distress has a good purpose, and God uses it to bring beauty, maturity, depth, and His grace into our lives. We also need to remember is that distress is not permanent. It has a time and a purpose. God used temporary negative circumstances to teach Naomi the value of others, the need for trust in God, and her purpose.

Ironically, distress is a good place to find God working in our lives. It is tempting to simply find a shortcut around distress, to seek to avoid any problems in life, to look for God in the wrong places, but we will see in the next chapter the danger of this approach to life. For now, take a few moments and consider how God might be seeking to restore your life through the distress you are experiencing. Can you begin, by faith, to see the value of your own distress?

CHAPTER 3

Elimelech's Bad Decision

As there is no earthly gain without some loss, so there is no worldly loss without some gain. If thou hast lost thy wealth, thou hast lost some trouble with it. If thou art degraded from thy honor, thou art likewise freed from the stroke of envy. If sickness hath blurred thy beauty, it hath delivered thee from pride. Set the allowance against the loss and thou shalt find no great loss.

Frances Quarles (1592–1644)

AS A BOY GROWING UP IN THE NORTHERN CALIfornia countryside, I would sometimes spy a bright shimmer through the clear water of a creek or stream, and my heart would skip a beat. I had found gold! I'd run to the metal, thinking about what I could buy with the bag of money that would surely result from my find. However, when I reached the source of the sparkle, I discovered that I had been fooled. The sparkly clump was nothing more than a pretty but worthless rock. I had found pyrite, or fool's gold.

The problem with fool's gold is that it looks like gold and glitters like gold, but it's not gold. Worse, fool's gold is so common in the earth's crust that it's found in almost every environment. Real gold is malleable—you can dent it with your fingernail—while pyrite is brittle. If you rub pyrite vigorously against a hard object, it gives off a sulphurous smell, like a rotten egg.

If only some of the foolish decisions we were planning to make were that easily identifiable.

Elimelech, like so many before and after him, fell for fool's gold. He was fooled by appearances and circumstances into believing that, contrary to what God had said, the grass really was greener on the other side of the fence. Moab looked good to Elimelech: there was no famine in Moab, and he wouldn't have to face the difficulty of life in Israel in Moab. Moving probably seemed like the obvious choice. Moab looked better, shinier, greener, but in the end it was merely a mirage, a spiritual forgery.

In this chapter we will see that it is easy to be fooled by appearances in life, and that we must be careful because we can make cataclysmic decisions based on assumptions that turn out to be false. We will see how a decision made by someone who was fooled by appearances changed the lives of many people.

FAMINE IN THE PROMISED LAND

Ruth 1:1–5 sets the scene for the entire book of Ruth, even though what we learn from the passage seems inconsequential. Yet, it is often the information that seems unimportant that yields the most valuable lessons.

> Now it came about in the days when the judges
> governed, that there was a famine in the land.
> And a certain man of Bethlehem in Judah went to
> sojourn in the land of Moab with his wife and his
> two sons. The name of the man was Elimelech, and
> the name of his wife, Naomi; and the names of his

two sons were Mahlon and Chilion, Ephrathites of Bethlehem in Judah. Now they entered the land of Moab and remained there. Then Elimelech, Naomi's husband, died; and she was left with her two sons. They took for themselves Moabite women as wives; the name of the one was Orpah and the name of the other Ruth. And they lived there about ten years. Then both Mahlon and Chilion also died, and the woman was bereft of her two children and her husband. (Ruth 1:1–5)

The very first line of the book of Ruth is a wealth of information and history: "Now it came about in the days when the judges governed, that there was a famine in the land." Here we have to ask ourselves a historical question: What land is the verse referring to? The answer is that the famine was in Israel. However, historically and scripturally, we are immediately faced with another question: Why was there famine in Israel? This was the land that God had given the Israelites. The land that He had given them was a land flowing with milk and honey, a good and a fertile land.

What had happened? Did God pull a bait and switch on them? Did He mislead them? The answer is found in the book of Leviticus in the Old Testament:

You shall not make for yourselves idols, nor shall you set up for yourselves an image or a sacred pillar, nor shall you place a figured stone in your land to bow down to it; for I am the LORD your God. You shall keep My sabbaths and reverence My sanctuary; I am the LORD. *If you walk in My statutes and keep My commandments so as to carry them out, then I shall give you rains in their season, so that the land will yield its produce and the trees of the field will bear their fruit. Indeed, your threshing will last for you until grape gathering, and grape gathering will last until sowing time. You will thus eat your food to the full and live securely in your land.* (Leviticus 26:1–5, emphasis added)

The covenant, or contract, that God had made with Israel that promised His blessing on the people of Israel and the land of Canaan was a *conditional* covenant. Both parties were responsible to do their part.

The most important condition was that the people of Israel would have no other gods before Him. In this same chapter God lays out what will happen if they disobey:

But if you do not obey Me and do not carry out all these commandments, if, instead, you reject My statutes, and if your soul abhors My ordinances so as not to carry out all My commandments, and so break My covenant, I, in turn, will do this to you: I will appoint over you a sudden terror, consumption and fever that will waste away the eyes and cause the soul to pine away; also, you will sow your seed uselessly, for your enemies will eat it up. I will set My face against you so that you will be struck down before your enemies; and those who hate you will rule over you, and you will flee when no one is pursuing you. If also after these things you do not obey Me, then I will punish you seven times more for your sins. I will also break down your pride of power; I will also make your sky like iron and your earth like bronze. *Your strength will be spent uselessly, for your land will not yield its produce and the trees of the land will not yield their fruit.* (Leviticus 26:14–20, emphasis added)

That first verse of Ruth tells us quite a bit after all, doesn't it? Remember that the book of Ruth occurred during the period of the judges, which was a period of terrible unfaithfulness by Israel toward God. Time after time the Israelites worshiped the god Baal instead of Jehovah. The Canaanite god Baal was believed to be owner of the land and to control its fertility.[1] This famine was no accident, nor freak of nature. This famine was a judgment of God on Israel for the people's disobedience because they were still under the covenant agreement.

The book of Ruth tells us that Elimelech decided to move from Israel to Moab to avoid the famine that was making life difficult in Israel. It certainly doesn't seem like he was doing anything out of the ordinary or important by moving, but his decision tells us about his faith, or maybe better, his faithlessness. In Deuteronomy 23:6, God tells the people of Israel regarding Moab, "You shall never seek their peace or their prosperity all your days." God clearly told Israel not to look for their livelihood and provision in Moab. Elimelech moved to Moab anyway.

Now Elimelech may have been a good man. It's not that he was evil, or didn't care for his family, or didn't have faith in or worship God. But we base every decision on principles we have come to believe, and we eventually begin to act on these principles without thinking. If the principles we base our decisions on aren't wise, the results of the decisions will often be bad. Every decision we make has the potential for consequences, and this was true of Elimelech's decision.

ELIMELECH NEGLECTED TO WAIT ON GOD'S PROMISES

Elimelech was doing what so many people do: he was looking for security in all the wrong places. He didn't believe that waiting on God to honor His promises was safer than disregarding them. Instead he sought security by circumventing the promises of God. Ironically, Elimelech's name meant "God is King," or "My God is King."[2] Names in ancient times reflected profound religious convictions. To name the name of God upon a child was to associate him in some way with God. Yet Elimelech didn't wait on God. David, who lived after Elimelech, says in Psalm 37:25, "I have been young, and now I am old, yet I have not seen the righteous forsaken or his descendants begging bread." God provides for those who wait, but Elimelech didn't give God the chance to act.

Living in the land of Israel, under the shelter of God, Elimelech did what is so tempting to do ourselves—leave the promises of God when things get difficult. Though I know it is wrong, I can find myself falling into the same trap. When it doesn't seem like God is going to answer my prayers exactly the way I expect Him to, in exactly the time I allot to Him, I am tempted to "fix" things myself. It is often easier to try to "fix" situations that God has ordained for us in our lives than to go through the difficult task of waiting on the Lord.

God displays His power most when we are most in need, but Elimelech didn't want to risk seeing if God would come through for him. Faith can seem like a risky proposition. What Elimelech didn't know was that waiting on the Lord would have turned out to be safer than going to Moab. As events unfolded, it is clear that Bethlehem in Israel, not Moab, was the place of blessing. Truly Moab was a fake. It promised everything and delivered nothing but despair and death to Elimelech.

The Discipline of Waiting

The Bible tells us over and over that God can be trusted in spite of how things look. God blessed David when he didn't kill King Saul, who was trying desperately to assassinate an innocent David out of jealousy. Even though several opportunities presented themselves, David waited on God to deliver Him and honor the promises He had made to him. David waited because he believed and trusted God.

Waiting on God is hard because circumstances seem to scream out to us that we need to fix things ourselves, forget the promises, and deliver ourselves. Maybe that's where you are today. You want your marriage fixed *now*. You want your finances fixed *now*. You want to find your husband or wife *now*. You want your confusion fixed *now*. You want your illness fixed *now*. You want all your problems to go away *now*. It is so hard to wait when the circumstances look bleak. We can so easily think: Maybe divorce is the answer. Maybe I should walk away from my financial responsibilities. Maybe I should give in to sexual temptation. Maybe I should get the abortion. Maybe the shortcut is the best answer. Maybe I should lie this time. When we don't see God working, we can grow resentful. We know He can do whatever He wants, but since He hasn't delivered us yet, we begin to judge His character and intentions.

Waiting on the Lord is hard because it involves the one thing we are all weak in—faith. Waiting on the Lord recognizes that God is at work on our behalf even when we can't see it. When we plant seeds, we have faith that plants will grow. We wait eagerly to see those plants finally break through the dirt. Much is going on while we wait, but the work is going on beneath the ground, invisible to our eyes. We see the results later.

Several years ago I wanted boysenberries in my garden, so I bought some vines and planted them, waiting for them to bloom and bear fruit. I was delighted when the vines finally began to leaf out, and then bloom—but I was so disappointed when they didn't bear any fruit. Not one single boysenberry! Wondering if perhaps I had done something wrong, I pulled out the booklet that had come with the vines. Lo and behold, there *was* something I hadn't read. The vines only *bloom* the first year; the second year the vines bear fruit. Nothing was wrong with the vine—it was doing exactly what it was supposed to be doing. I had to be patient, and frankly, that's not always one of my virtues. But I had little choice. I had to wait an entire year, but the next year I had enough boysenberries to make a pie! And I had gained wisdom. There are times in our lives when we just need to wait to allow God's promises to bear fruit.

An important lesson from the life of Elimelech is that waiting on God to honor His promises is safer than disregarding them, or trying to circumvent them by other routes. Elimelech applied conventional wisdom to the problem he faced. We do it all the time without thinking. We begin with the need: I need money. I need to be healed. I need courage. I need a relationship. I need something to happen. I need something to go away. Then in our limited wisdom we try to figure out how God might meet the need. Personally, I know God has promised to help me, and that He has told me to cling to His promises and to pray, but when I do that and don't get any quick relief I get nervous because, well, I'm a great fan of quick relief! So ultimately, if my faith grows weak, I try to find some way to fix the situation. I leave Israel, the place of promise, and go to Moab, the place of self-determination. I leave the promises of God and chase conventional wisdom. At times following conventional wisdom and ignoring the promises of God sounds easier and safer.

In the heady days of the stock market's rapid growth in the late '90s and early 2000s, investors encouraged people to place their money in a number of dot-coms, Web-based or Web-dependent businesses that were seeing meteoric gains. The cataclysmic failures of

WorldCom and Enron—failures that affected millions—have made the company names bywords for the excess of that time and show that conventional wisdom is not always trustworthy. Real estate was the next moneymaker, and everyone rushed to get in on the real estate market, often buying homes with risky loans. Everyone was doing it, but not everyone could afford it. Our country's financial system nearly collapsed. God promised Abraham a son, but as time went on, Sarah thought the process needed help—so she gave her husband her handmaiden to produce a son (see Genesis 16). The conflict between the descendants of Abraham's sons continues today. Conventional wisdom always sounds good *at the time*—that's why it's so attractive. The words of God, on the other hand, can sound so ancient and out of date, but only in them can we find eternal truth.

The life of Elimelech reminds us that we need to wait on God to honor His promises. There are many stories of how God miraculously met the needs of His people in times of famine and need. God knew Elimelech's address, and friends, He knows yours! His promises can and will be kept, in His time and in His way. That's what the promises of God are, our refuge, our guarantee from God.

Many of us make promises we can't keep. We mean to keep them, but one day find out that we can't do what we promised. God's promises are not like that. Only God can make a promise He can always keep, in every situation, through every circumstance, no matter what! Elimelech missed an opportunity to see God work greatly through negative circumstances. God cares for those who love Him and seek Him.

The Discipline of Trusting

How do you approach the promises of God? The story is told that in the early days of our country a weary traveler came to the banks of the Mississippi River for the very first time. There was no bridge to cross and it was early winter. The river was covered with ice, but was the ice strong enough to hold him? He had no way of knowing. Night was falling, and he had to get to the other side. Finally, after much inward struggling and with great fear and trepidation, he got on his hands and knees and crawled cautiously onto the ice, trying to distribute his weight as much as possible. He was halfway across the river, scared to death and wondering if at any moment he might break through and drown, when he heard the sound of singing behind him. Turning around, he saw in the dim light of dusk a man coming toward him in a horse-drawn wagon. The driver never wavered or paused, but drove the horse and heavily laden wagon across the ice singing merrily at the top of his lungs.[3]

You can imagine the relief that flooded the man as he was able to stand on the surface he had only recently been afraid to crawl on. This is such an apt picture of how some of us struggle with the promises of God. We hesitate and wonder with great trepidation if we can trust God. We have learned to step tentatively in anxious concern upon the promises of God, as if our light steps make it easier for God to help us, when God would much rather have us run and jump out upon His promises with conviction and courage and hope. D. L. Moody, the great evangelist of the last century, once said, "God never made a promise that was too good to be true."[4] Sometimes the problem with trusting in God's promises is that they seem too good to be true. But they're not.

ELIMELECH GAVE IN TO TEMPTATION

Ruth 1:1 tells us that Elimelech "went to sojourn in the land of Moab with his wife and his two sons." The word *sojourn* is interesting because it indicates that Elimelech never intended this trip to be permanent. He was planning to stay only until the situation got better back home. How long was he planning to stay in Moab—a few months, a few years? We're not sure when Elimelech died into this sojourn, but it seems clear he did not expect to be buried in Moab. Would he have gone if he had known the result?

The life of sojourners, or migrants in a foreign land, wasn't the easiest kind of life. The Israelites were prohibited from buying or owning land in Moab. This left few options, one being working for low wages for someone else. But at the time, it might have looked better than famine in Israel.

How we struggle with this same issue. The grass is greener on the other side of the fence. Moab looked good compared to Israel. That was Elimelech's temptation, but we are tempted the same way. When trouble comes into our lives, usually the first thing we are looking for is the escape hatch. We don't pause to ask ourselves, What is God trying to teach me through this? or, How might this experience be used by God to strengthen my faith or transform me more into the image of Jesus Christ? We just want to make it go away! We are tempted to leave God's plan and go after something else. Immorality starts looking better than holiness. That other person starts looking better than my spouse. Dishonesty starts looking more rewarding than honesty and integrity. Bitterness starts looking better than forgiveness. Compromise starts looking better than faithfulness to God.

It is tempting to do things we know we shouldn't and justify our actions with the thought that we're not going to keep it up, it's only temporary. Elimelech's actions give us a warning we should heed: temporary deviations from God's plan can easily lead to permanent migrations. Alcoholics start with one drink. Those trapped in substance abuse start with "just trying it." A young person who feels in love engages in sexual activity outside of marriage "just this once." A person clicks on to an online pornography site just to see what all the fuss is about. They are later appalled at what they did and feel terrible regret. But it's easier the second time. It's always easier the second time. Then the trap snaps shut. As C. S. Lewis wrote,

> Good and evil both increase at compound interest. That is why the little decisions you and I make every day are of such infinite importance. The smallest good act today is the capture of a strategic point from which, a few months later, you may be able to go on to victories you never dreamed of. An apparently trivial indulgence in lust or anger today is the loss of a ridge or railway line or bridgehead from which the enemy may launch an attack otherwise impossible.[5]

Years ago an accountant in my city pilfered the Little League bank account he was entrusted with. He took thousands of dollars. He didn't start with the intention of stealing from little boys, but he got into a financial jam at home and took a shortcut. He intended to pay back the money, and he never intended to keep it up, but the first time he did it made it easier the second time and the third time until he was in so deep there was no way out. He had financial problems, the kind we all face, but he took a temporary and dangerous migration that led him to a permanent address—prison. He lost his home and everything that was important to him and gained only disgrace and shame.

Elimelech's final stop was Moab. He never meant it to be. His sons both died in Moab. His wife was left destitute in a foreign land. His temporary sojourn turned permanent. Going to Moab seemed like such a good idea at the time. It probably seemed like the safe thing to do. But God had told the Israelites not to do what Elimelech was planning to do. Elimelech gave in to temptation and deviated from God's plan.

Are you in the midst of taking a temporary deviation from God's will and plan? Have you given in to temptation? It's not too late to stop and make a change. It might be too late tomorrow. Act now. The bad place you are in is still escapable, but there may come a time when it isn't. The consequences may become too great. You may have to face penalties because of your actions, but a freeing truth you can cling to is that it is never too late to start doing what is right.

Never.

ELIMELECH HINDERED GOD'S FLOW OF BLESSINGS TO OTHERS

Ruth 1:2 tells us that Elimelech was an "Ephrathite of Bethlehem in Judah." Ephratha was the original name of Bethlehem.[6] Saying it was in Judah differentiated it from another northern town called Bethlehem. It is possible that this designation was given to Elimelech to tell us that he was from an old established family in Bethlehem, possibly that he was part of the local hierarchy. His family had lived there and survived there for years. Elimelech's decision to move may have had a profound effect on his community. We know for certain that his decision affected his immediate family.

Everything we do affects other people. So often we act as if this isn't true, but it is! Unfortunately our bad decisions can be most costly to those closest to us. Elimelech didn't go to Moab alone, he took his wife, Naomi, and his two sons, Mahlon and Chilion. But in this move Elimelech hindered the flow of God's blessing to his loved ones.

I am sure Elimelech had no idea the effect his "quick fix" decision would have on his family, particularly his sons. Elimelech "quick fixed" his problem, so when his sons wanted to marry, they "quick fixed" the situation too. They neglected God's promises, just as their father had. Deuteronomy 23:3–4 says,

> No Ammonite or Moabite shall enter the assembly
> of the LORD; none of their descendants, even to the
> tenth generation, shall ever enter the assembly of
> the LORD, because they did not meet you with food
> and water on the way when you came out of Egypt,
> and because they hired against you Balaam the son
> of Beor from Pethor of Mesopotamia, to curse you.

It's clear where Moab stood according to the law,[7] but let's look again at verse 6: "You shall never seek their peace or their prosperity all your days." The Israelites knew that they were not to look to Moab for their livelihood and provision. Elimelech sought the prosperity of Moab, and his sons learned from Dad. Elimelech's sons could have gone back to Israel to find wives, but they chose not to. We can find peace and prosperity right here in Moab, they reasoned. We can even find wives here. After all, we're locals now!

The effect Elimelech's decision had on Naomi would probably have pained him had he known about it. She stayed in Moab only because her sons married Moabite women. When her husband and sons died, she was left alone in a strange place with strange customs and a strange religion.

Elimelech's "quick fix" hindered Naomi and his sons from experiencing the blessings promised to Israel. In fact, Naomi left Moab because God blessed Israel greatly with food. Elimelech didn't need to change his address; God knew where He lived. God's provision would have found him, God's care would have found him, and God's promises would have found him. God honors those who honor Him.

There are times when we need to ask ourselves, How are my decisions affecting those closest to me? What am I training my children to do? What am I modeling for my wife or husband? What example does my action set for others? Would I want them doing what I'm doing, trusting in what I'm trusting in, loving what I'm loving? Jon Mohr wrote a beautiful song titled "Find Us Faithful."[8] The lyrics challenge us on this point:

We're pilgrims on the journey
Of the narrow road
And those who've gone before us line the way
Cheering on the faithful, encouraging the weary
Their lives a stirring testament to God's sustaining grace

Surrounded by so great a cloud of witnesses
Let us run the race not only for the prize
But as those who've gone before us
Let us leave to those behind us
The heritage of faithfulness
Passed on through godly lives

Oh may all who come behind us find us faithful
May the fire of our devotion light their way
May the footprints that we leave
Lead them to believe
And the lives we live inspire them to obey
Oh may all who come behind us find us faithful

After all our hopes and dreams have come and gone
And our children sift through all we've left behind
May the clues that they discover
And the memories they uncover
Become the light that leads them
To the road we each must find

Oh may all who come behind us find us faithful

The decisions we make affect others, and we are leaving a legacy even now. Is it going to be a legacy of faith, or a legacy of faithlessness? Will my life point others to God and trust in Him, or away from God and away from trust in Him? We must be careful because our actions can hinder the flow of God's blessings to our loved ones.

ELIMELECH SENT A MESSAGE WITH HIS ACTIONS

We learn from Elimelech's example that our actions often send messages our mouths never would! Moab and Israel were enemies. They worshiped different gods. What kind of message must the Moabites have received when Elimelech left the Promised Land and the promises of the God of Israel to turn to Moab for his security? The answer is simple: the God of Israel can't provide for His people anymore, but our god Chemosh can! Elimelech's Hebrew family became great propaganda for the cause of Chemosh, god of the Moabites!

Elimelech would never have said that, but his actions did! I've noticed the potential for this problem in my life. I don't often take into account how what I do looks to those who don't yet know my Lord. Do I talk about trusting and faith, and then take actions that show that I have neither? Do I talk about the importance of allowing God to work in my life in whatever way He wants to, and then when He does, spend all my time complaining? Do I talk about loving my brother and sister and forgiving them, and then when somebody hurts me, find some way to get even? Few of us would verbally say,

- I don't trust God with this issue.
- I don't think God knows what He's doing right now.
- I don't forgive them, I'm going to get even.
- I don't believe God can fix this, it's too messed up even for Him.

- Faith is not a good bet, you can't depend on God.

. . . but sometimes our actions send messages that our mouths never would.

We say that we trust God—but then proceed to spend our time worrying aloud about how things are going to turn out. What message are we sending? We say that everything we have belongs to God—but if He takes some of it away, we start complaining and get depressed. What message are we sending?

Years ago in Germany there was a young Jewish boy who had a profound sense of admiration for his father. The life of the family centered on the acts of piety and devotion prescribed by their religion. The father was zealous in attending worship and instruction and demanded the same from his children. When the boy was a teenager, the family was forced to move to another town in Germany. There was no synagogue in the new location, and the pillars of the community all belonged to the Lutheran church. Suddenly the father announced to the family that they were going to abandon their Jewish traditions and join the Lutheran church. When the stunned family asked why, the father explained that it was necessary to help his business. The youngster was bewildered and confused. His deep disappointment soon gave way to anger and a kind of intense bitterness that plagued him throughout his life.

He left Germany and went to England to study. He sat daily at the British Museum formulating his ideas and composing a book. In that book, he conceived of a movement that was designed to change the world, and he described religion as an "opiate for the masses" that could be explained totally in terms of economics. Today billions of people live under the system invented by this embittered man. His name, of course, is Karl Marx. The influence of this father's hypocrisy is still being felt around the world.[9]

Karl Marx got the message from his father loud and clear: religion wasn't about loving and serving God, it was about staying connected to the right people for economic reasons. His father's religion was just a pose.

ARE WE TRYING TO CIRCUMVENT GOD'S PLANS?

St. Ambrose, writing over a thousand years ago, said, "Our whole Roman world had gone dead in its heart because it feared tragedy, took flight from suffering, and abhorred failure. In fear of failure we worshiped power. In fear of suffering, we worshiped security. During the rising splendor of our thousand years, we had grown cruel, practical, and sterile. We did win the whole world, but in the process, we lost our souls."[10]

God can meet us right where we are. We do not need to fear tragedy or suffering, or failure, for He can deliver us from all these things. He knows your address, and He knows what you are suffering even now. Anything that takes the place of trust in God is a forgery—just spiritual fool's gold. As you look at your situation, lean on the promises of God and keep a careful eye out for forgeries.

Can you think of a promise of God that you are trying to hurry up, "quick fix," or circumvent to get what you want without the waiting? Waiting on God to honor His promises is safer than disregarding them. What He says He will do, He will do, in the perfect time.

Is there an area in your life where you have temporarily deviated from what you know to be God's plan? Be careful, you could end up with a new permanent address! Safety is factored into God's plan for your life, but not so your own plans. God's plans for us are perfect and based on eternal truths, but ours are not—they are often based on feelings and guesses.

Is there an area in your life in which your actions could be hindering the flow of God's blessings to your spouse, children, friends, and relatives? Can you take that ultimate step of selfless love and stop those actions for the sake of those closest to you?

Are your actions sending messages that your mouth never would? Most of these messages we don't intend to send. Can we take the difficult steps of identifying these messages and changing behavior to reflect a partnership between what we say and what we do?

The life of Elimelech prompts us to ask ourselves what we really believe about God. Not what we *say* we believe, but what we really believe. God made His will known to Elimelech, but Elimelech chose to ignore God and it cost him and his family. The Elimelechs of the Bible are there not for us to ridicule, but so we can learn from them. God doesn't want us making those same mistakes.

God is restoring us into something authentic, real, and holy—and we must be on guard in our lives for those temptations to take shortcuts that derail our restoration. Partial restoration is not God's purpose in our lives. He wants to restore every part of us. When God gets done with us we should hope to hear others say one day, "We found them faithful!"

CHAPTER 4

Ruth's Godly Example

*The main business of friendship is to sustain and
make bearable each other's burdens. We may do
more of that as friends than we do anything else.*

Eugene Kennedy

AN AMAZING FACT OF OUR CREATION IS THAT NO
two people are alike. God in His infinite wisdom and creativity
managed to make every single person different from every other person in history. We may share some characteristics with others, but
always with variations that make us unique and special.

We are told that snowflakes are unique too. Their uniqueness
comes from being pushed around in the turbulence of the wind.
During this process, each crystal experiences a different temperature
and humidity, and as a result the crystals melt, grow, partly evapo-
rate, or even break while bouncing into other crystals.[1] In a similar
way, surely the turbulence of life shapes each person's God-given and
unique personality and creates unique people with unique strengths
and challenges.

Because each of us is uniquely made, God brings into our lives
those people who can uniquely meet our specific needs. These people
complement our lives; they are the missing pieces to the puzzle of
life we face. They were specially designed by God to be just what we

need to mature and grow in our faith, and He brings them to us just when we need them. These special people complement our strengths and challenge our weaknesses. They bring balance and maturity into our lives in a way no one else could because they are often so very different than we are. They look different, talk different, have different backgrounds, look at life differently than we do, and even think differently than we do.

When we look for friendships, we usually search for people who are like us, but God doesn't. We want people who have the same kind of spiritual or emotional holes that we have in our lives, but God wants to bring us godly examples who complement us and help to repair us. Tragically, because of immaturity, or ignorance, or pain, we often fail to appreciate these people or even recognize them. In fact, sometimes God brings people into our lives and we try to return them, as Naomi did with Ruth. But God, in His wonderful mercy and loyal loving-kindness, gently insists that there are *no refunds*. God designed these "specialty people" to be the channel of great blessings. They can help us grow and blossom . . . if we allow it!

As we observe Ruth and Naomi, we see why these specialty people are necessary to us and how God uses them to restore us. Our specialty people challenge us to nobler ambitions, remain committed to us, model attitudes we lack, and provide a needed perspective. Hopefully, by the end of the chapter, you will be able to identify the specialty people God has brought into your life and begin to appreciate and accept their impact on you.

RUTH CHALLENGED NAOMI TO NOBLER AMBITIONS

Our specialty people are necessary to us because they challenge us to nobler ambitions! Ruth provided such a challenge to Naomi. In 1:6–9 we see both Orpah and Ruth had started to accompany Naomi home. It was likely an act of Oriental courtesy for Ruth and

Orpah to follow Naomi to the border.[2] Returning the courtesy, she urged them to go home: "Go, return each of you to her mother's house. May the LORD deal kindly with you as you have dealt with the dead and with me. May the LORD grant that you may find rest, each in the house of her husband."

She prayed that the Lord would grant her daughters-in-law rest. This word *rest* is the Hebrew word *menuchah*. It speaks of a rest, not in the ordinary sense of relief from work, but of a safe shelter, a protection. This is the word Hebrews used to speak of a husband's house. It was a woman's rest, safe resort, protection, and security.[3]

In the ancient Near East, a woman without a husband was in a serious situation, because she lacked literal security. She had no one to protect her, she was socially shamed, and she had no real role in society apart from a husband and children. Naomi was trying to be noble herself, but in the midst of her pain, her judgment was not very clear. She simply wanted what was best for Orpah and Ruth, who had been good to her and her sons. If her daughters-in-law stayed in Moab, being Moabite women, the prospect of finding husbands and having children was good. Naomi knew the prospect of finding Jewish men to marry them in Israel was poor, and she tried to persuade them that following her was not a good option. Naomi was trying to achieve external security for Ruth and Orpah, the kind of security this world provides.

In Naomi's distress it probably didn't occur to her that marrying Elimelech had only provided "rest" while he was alive, and his and their sons' death left her destitute. What marriage provided was temporary security at best. Ruth chose to look at security with a different perspective. Naomi had found her rest in marriage to Elimelech, but Ruth sought her rest in Jehovah. In verse 16, Ruth made the grand confession to Naomi that Naomi's God would be her God. That was not a statement she made lightly. She understood fully the implications of what she was saying.

Ruth was looking for a more permanent security than marriage could provide. Her husband had died as well, so she knew the temporary nature of that kind of security and was seeking something more permanent. Naomi's ambition had been noble, to try and get a better life for her daughters-in-law, but Ruth's had been nobler, to find her security, protection, and safe haven in Jehovah and not in a man. Later we will see that Boaz recognized that truth when he says to Ruth, "May the LORD reward your work, and your wages be full from the LORD, the God of Israel, under whose wings you have come to seek refuge" (2:12).

Specialty people in our lives challenge us to nobler ambitions than our own. Sometimes our goals are too low and not worthy of our Lord. Specialty people help to raise our sights. Not only did Ruth confess her reliance on Naomi's God, she demonstrated it to Naomi by leaving her homeland and every prospect for remarriage to accompany her.

The story is told of King Henry III of Bavaria, who in the eleventh century grew tired and weary of court life and the pressures of ruling. He applied to Prior Richard at a local monastery to be accepted as a contemplative and spend the rest of his life in the monastery. Prior Richard questioned King Henry about his decision.

"Your Majesty," said Prior Richard, "do you understand that the pledge here is one of obedience? That will be hard because you have been a king."

"I understand," said Henry. "The rest of my life I will be obedient to you, as Christ leads you."

"Then I will tell you what to do," said Prior Richard. "Go back to your throne and serve faithfully in the place where God has put you." King Henry did as he was told, and when he died a statement was read: "The king learned to rule by being obedient."

Ruth served faithfully in the situation and place where God had put her, even though it entailed difficulty. Naomi, even in her distress, must have noticed Ruth's response and faithfulness to God, and Ruth's example challenged Naomi to nobler ambitions.

I have a number of specialty people in my life, some I recognize as such, and some I am sure I don't. They see strengths in me that I don't and remind me of my calling when I grow weary. They keep me focused on what I'm supposed to be focused on. They are not pastors or authors like me, but people who are often the opposite of me, like puzzle pieces of the opposite shape that fit together perfectly.

My wife is one such person. As a young man I had lofty goals and grandiose visions, most totally unrealistic, but tantalizing. They often drove me. Annette's desires are usually so very simple. It doesn't take much to make her happy. What is really important in life is really important to her, and what isn't as important isn't a priority to her. I wish I was more like her, which is why I so desperately need her influence. Like Ruth provided a nobler ambition for Naomi and challenged her outlook, so the specialty people that God has provided for us challenge us to nobler ambitions. They often see more potential in our lives than we do and encourage us to realize it.

My specialty people include an engineer; a young, inexperienced pastor; an older, more experienced pastor; an elderly, mentally retarded man; my own children; and other family members, each of whom, in their own way, challenged me to nobler ambitions.

RUTH REMAINED COMMITTED TO NAOMI

Most of us who watched the 2008 Summer Olympics remember Jason Lezak's sensational swim as anchor of the victorious U.S. 400-meter freestyle relay team. What you might not know is that Lezak, the oldest U.S. male Olympic swimmer at age thirty-two, took a long trail of ups and downs to arrive in Beijing. His world-class body blossomed during his junior year at the University of California at Santa Barbara, but he was kicked off the team by Coach Gregg Wilson because of a bad attitude. This was difficult for Gregg Wilson. I know—he's a friend of mine. He goes to my church. Gregg is an amazingly encouraging and positive personality. Yet, for the good of the team, he had to do it. But it's not like Gregg to give up on someone when they can still be won over. He cares deeply about all his athletes. After talking to his swimmer, he convinced Lezak to sign a behavioral contract and apologize to his teammates. Only then did Gregg let him back on the team. Later Lezak said, "I learned an important lesson, that I wasn't bigger than the team."[4] Gregg Wilson remained committed to Lezak even when Lezak made it difficult. Such people are invaluable to each of us.

I'd like to call your attention to a very important word that occurs a number of times in 1:8–15. This word is uttered by Naomi to Orpah and Ruth, and then finally just to Ruth. In these verses the word that repeats is the word *return*:

> And Naomi said to her two daughters-in-law, "Go, *return* each of you to her mother's house . . ." Then she kissed them, and they lifted up their voices and wept. And they said to her, "No, but we will surely *return* with you to your people." But Naomi said, "*Return*, my daughters. Why should you go with me? Have I yet sons in my womb, that they may be your husbands? *Return*, my daughters! Go, for I am too old to have a husband. If I said I have hope, if I should even have a husband tonight and also bear sons, would you therefore wait until they were grown? Would you therefore refrain from marrying? No, my daughters; for it is harder for me than for you, for the hand of the LORD has gone forth against

me." And they lifted up their voices and wept again; and Orpah kissed her mother-in-law, but Ruth clung to her. Then she said, "Behold, your sister-in-law has gone back to her people and her gods; *return* after your sister-in-law." (emphasis added)

Four times in a short dialogue Naomi tries to convince Ruth to leave her. The development of her arguments hints that her attitude and even volume might have become increasingly sharp and biting. There is a hint of exasperation in Naomi's words that must have come across to Ruth.

This scene reminds me of the irritation I've seen in some people when, in their pain, they try to get you to leave them, and they blurt out in exasperation, "Look, I just need to be alone, OK?" I have noticed that people will do this in times of distress to test the commitment of those closest to them. They try to push people away to see if they will go. They don't want them to go—they actually desperately want them to stay—but they don't want them to stay unless they really want to. Distressed people don't want pity, they want true friends, but in their pain they don't know how to say that, so they act it out.

The context and dialogue make it clear that Naomi was definitely hurting. She was grieving, self-absorbed (as we will see), insensitive, and generally not much fun to be around. Few truly hurting people are. Naomi did not make it easy for Ruth to be committed to her. She did everything she possibly could to make it difficult, but God wouldn't let Naomi get rid of Ruth!

Some people we try to push away from us go gladly and quickly, but our specialty people, those tailor-made for us by God, refuse to leave, even though we likely have given them more reason to go than anyone. Their love and commitment to us is not dependent upon our always being "up" or our outlook being good. Ruth would not let Naomi push her away. Ruth knew that Naomi needed her. Her commitment to Naomi was part of her commitment to God. Naomi's protestations could not sway her; she knew her place was with Naomi, no matter what.

I thank God for those people who have stood by me in my ugly moments and in the difficult periods of my life. I can see that they were tailor-made for me, because they remained committed to me, even when I made it difficult.

RUTH MODELED ATTITUDES NAOMI LACKED

Ruth modeled attitudes Naomi lacked. Notice I said *modeled*, not preached. There is no shortage of people who want to *preach* the right attitudes to us, but precious few who *model* them—quietly, gently and with great patience and tolerance. May they indeed inherit the earth.

In 1:10–13 we read of Orpah's and Ruth's desire to remain with their mother-in-law. But Naomi, pointing out what that meant for them and the foolishness of that decision, began to make her case. She referred to the Levirate custom in Israel in which a brother was responsible to marry his deceased brother's wife in order to conceive a son and perpetuate his brother's name and inheritance. God tells the nation of Israel in Deuteronomy 25:5–6:

> When brothers live together and one of them dies
> and has no son, the wife of the deceased shall not
> be married outside the family to a strange man.
> Her husband's brother shall go in to her and
> take her to himself as wife and perform the duty
> of a husband's brother to her. It shall be that the
> firstborn whom she bears shall assume the name of

his dead brother, that his name will not be blotted
out from Israel.

Naomi points out that this custom, if they were placing any hope
in it, was useless at this point. She was too old to marry. And even
if she married that day, and through a miracle had twin sons nine
months later, it would be many, many years before the sons were of a
marrying age, and it would be silly for them to wait for that. She was
basically saying, "Look, what are you going to do, wait around for
twenty years until my sons are grown? That's just crazy. Go home."

Naomi urged them to return to their homes and gods where they
would have a chance to remarry and have a family. But in verse 13,
she said something rather insensitive. At the end of her arguments, she
said, "No, my daughters; for it is harder [literally, "more bitter"] for
me than for you, for the hand of the LORD has gone forth against me."

Naomi was not sensitive to the grief of her daughters-in-law, who
were also recent widows. She argued that her case was more bitter
than theirs because they still had the potential for child bearing and
marrying. She didn't. But in reflection, who had it worse? Naomi,
who could not marry or have children, or Ruth, who could do both,
but voluntarily gave them up out of love for Naomi and God?

Did Naomi lose her husband? So did Ruth. Did Naomi's future
look bleak? So did Ruth's, especially by staying with Naomi. Was
Naomi without any children? So was Ruth, and staying with Naomi
was the cause of it. Did Naomi lack security? So did Ruth. Had
Naomi left her country, Ruth was going to do the same thing, except
not for a period of years, but forever. Naomi had no choice over her
circumstances; Ruth did. Not only did Ruth give it up, she begged
for the opportunity! She even put herself under a curse from God
if she didn't live up to her commitment to Naomi. She told Naomi,
"Do not urge me to leave you or turn back from following you; for
where you go, I will go, and where you lodge, I will lodge. Your

people shall be my people, and your God, my God. Where you die, I will die, and there I will be buried. Thus may the LORD do to me, and worse, if anything but death parts you and me" (1:16–17).

Later Ruth, standing by Naomi, heard Naomi speak to the women of Bethlehem who were buzzing with excitement as they saw Naomi returning. It's clear Naomi had been well known to them. But this was not the same Naomi they had known, and she confirmed it to them: "Do not call me Naomi (pleasant); call me Mara (bitter), for the Almighty has dealt very bitterly with me. I went out full, but the LORD has brought me back empty. Why do you call me Naomi, since the Lord has witnessed against me and the Almighty has afflicted me?" (1:20–21).

I find it illuminating that we don't see Ruth standing by Naomi, chiming in with, "Yeah, call me Mara as well; my life's also a complete bust. Just look at what God has done to us—aren't we a mess? Just call us the bitter twins. Life stinks, and then you die!" We don't see Ruth sticking out her hand and saying, "Hello, I'm Naomi's friend. You can call me 'Empty.' The Lord brought me back with Naomi. Are we pathetic or what?"

What is conspicuously lacking in the biblical account is any complaining on Ruth's part about her reduced circumstances. Naomi, forgetting her faith for a moment, complained, but we hear not a peep from Ruth. In this, Ruth shined brighter in her newfound faith than Naomi, who introduced her to this faith. Ruth never said, "God has dealt with me bitterly," and yet she lost and gave up everything, even more than Naomi had.

This is what our specialty people do. Their godly attitude shames us and encourages us to see our situation differently. They politely and gently decline to attend our pity parties. How God can use these people in our lives if we allow Him to!

Strangely, we don't often respond well to the incredible example of our specialty people. It can grate on us when those near us choose not to join us in expressing our misery, especially when they have a comparable or a greater reason than us to be miserable. Faced with the same kind of situation—maybe worse—they maintain a remarkable attitude and outlook. They don't push their attitude on us, either; they just quietly model it to us.

Ruth remained silent, but her quiet actions and commitment modeled attitudes that Naomi could not produce. Our specialty people model attitudes we sorely lack, and though they often have more reason to complain than we do, they remain patiently quiet.

RUTH PROVIDED NAOMI WITH A NEEDED PERSPECTIVE

Specialty people remember what we forget and appreciate more fully what we often take for granted. They provide a perspective that we can no longer see. How, knowing the pain she must have felt herself, could Ruth have made her famous statement, "Where you go I will go, and where you lodge, I will lodge. Your people shall be my people, and your God, my God. Where you die, I will die, and there I will be buried" (1:16–17)? The clear reason is that she gave her heart fully and unreservedly to Jehovah, and compared to that joy, all other things were loss. Paul echoed her perspective when he wrote in Philippians, "But whatever things were gain to me, those things I have counted as loss for the sake of Christ. More than that, I count all things to be loss in view of the surpassing value of knowing Christ Jesus my Lord, for whom I have suffered the loss of all things, and count them but rubbish so that I may gain Christ" (3:7–8).

Naomi, being Jewish all her life, had for the moment taken that relationship with God for granted, but Ruth was like the woman at the well, tasting the living water of Jesus for the first time (see John 4:1–42). In reality, what Ruth was saying to Naomi by her actions, when Naomi was trying to get her to go home was, "Naomi, *I am home.* Jehovah is my home now. He's my rest, my protection, and my shelter. You showed me that. You gave me a greater gift than my own family. They gave me physical life, but you have shown me how to find eternal life. They offered me temporary security, as did my husband, but Jehovah provides me eternal security."

Those who have not grown up with an understanding of the reality of God, who have not grown up in church nor been around Christianity, are often the quickest to receive it to heart, and the most passionately committed to it. To try to bring this into perspective, let's imagine a couple who live on the shore of a great lake. Both the husband and the wife appreciate the lake's magnificent beauty. The husband was brought there as a child and has lived there his whole life. It was all he ever knew. The sight of the lake is familiar. The wife grew up in an arid desert. She could never remember a time when she wasn't thirsty, or when water was plentiful. Memories of thirst and a parched throat still linger in her mind. When the man married the woman, they moved into the house on the lake.

Whenever the couple look upon the lake, they are reminded of how fortunate they are to live there. Certainly they both appreciate their lake home, but who do you think appreciates it more? Who continually marvels at it more, and is less likely to go in search of another place to live? Who will never take for granted the blessedness of the view from their house?

Ruth knew that her options were severely limited when she followed Naomi. So it is clear that her decision to follow Naomi, and her God, was based on something she felt she had already received, not anything material that lay before her. From the limited ability to look into the future that Ruth had, she had to be firmly convinced that

- Her options were going to be 0.
- Her assets were going to be 0.

- Her friends and family (other than Naomi) were going to be 0.
- Her potential prospects were going to be 0.

This is the essence of someone who has a real relationship with God. The love and joy in the relationship with God is based on something He has already given the person, not on what he or she hopes to ultimately get out of the arrangement. *He is enough.*

In this case the convert saw the issue of conversion more clearly than did the evangelist. Naomi wanted Ruth to return to Chemosh, but Ruth realized that there was no turning back. After a difficult teaching, when many of Jesus' disciples left Him, He turned to his twelve disciples and asked them if they were going to leave also. Peter replied, "Lord, to whom shall we go? You have words of eternal life. We have believed and have come to know that You are the Holy One of God" (John 6:68–69). Ruth did not want to go back to her nation's gods after learning about the amazing God of Israel. In this, Naomi the evangelist received lessons from Ruth the disciple.

Naomi's return to Israel was seen in her eyes in terms of loss. Ruth's going to Israel was seen in her eyes as gain. They were both going to the same place and would endure the same difficult circumstances, but how different were their perspectives about it?

WHO ARE YOUR SPECIALTY PEOPLE?

Specialty people challenge us to nobler ambitions; remain committed to us, even when we make it difficult; model attitudes we sorely lack; and provide a needed perspective in our lives.

Who are your specialty people? Who has challenged you with nobler ambitions? Who has remained committed to you, even when by words or actions you have made that difficult? Who has modeled attitudes you sorely lack? Who provides a different perspective in your life? Have you been resisting their efforts? Have you even resented them? God graciously provided these people for you. Let them affect you.

One of the tender, compassionate ways that God restores us is by sending us special, made-to-order, one-of-a-kind friends. Let us not turn them away or turn away from them. We were not meant to bear our pain and our load alone. When we have been hurt and are distressed and stumbling badly, those who have walked with God, those who He has restored through their own distress, are waiting in the shadows of our lives to help us walk again.

That's pretty special.

CHAPTER 5

Naomi's Reappraisal of God's Character

Take those road hazards—the potholes, ruts, detours, and all the rest—as evidence that you're on the right route. It's when you find yourself on that big, broad, easy road that you ought to worry.

Joni Eareckson Tada

SCHOLAR, AUTHOR, AND PHILOSOPHER C. S. LEWIS was briefly married when he was in his late fifties to Joy Davidman, a divorced American mother of two boys whose previous husband was an alcoholic and frequent adulterer. Her slow conversion from atheism to faith had been encouraged from afar by Lewis's books, and through a series of events, she had an opportunity to meet Lewis in England in 1950. In the course of their friendship, she revealed her difficulties to Lewis, who listened, grieved for her, and said a sad farewell in January of 1951 as she returned to her difficult situation in the States.

Unable to reconcile with her husband, who refused to abandon his adulterous ways, she returned to England with her boys, and her husband sued her for divorce. For almost two years, Lewis and Joy grew closer as friends. However, in 1956, the British government refused to renew Joy's visa. Lewis struggled with his dear friend having to go back to a horrible situation in the States. So, to avoid her forced return, he married Joy in a civil ceremony later that year, though they did not live together as man and wife. He sought a sacramental marriage in the Anglican church but was refused because Davidman had been divorced, even though her husband had been repeatedly adulterous, and she had become a Christian after these events.

In 1957, Joy fell in her kitchen and broke her leg. Tragically, X-rays revealed that she had cancer throughout her body. She was given a few days, perhaps weeks, to live. Lewis sought out an Anglican priest willing to marry them in the church, and in 1957, he and Joy were married in the Anglican church. Though she moved into his home expecting to die, miraculously, Joy's cancer went into remission for three years. By now, the two were deeply in love and constantly at each other's side. Writing to a friend at the time, Lewis said, "It's funny having at 59 the sort of happiness most men have in their twenties . . . Thou has kept the good wine until now." Sadly, the cancer returned with a vengeance in 1960. Joy died in the spring of that year.[1]

In his book *A Grief Observed*, Lewis, referring to his wife's death and the way that event challenged his relationship with God, wrote, "Not that I am (I think) in much danger of ceasing to believe in God. The real danger is of coming to believe such dreadful things about Him. The conclusion I dread is not 'So there's no God after all,' but 'So this is what God's really like. Deceive yourself no longer.'"[2]

God forces us to reexamine His character when we are in pain. Rather than trying to hide in divine embarrassment over the circumstances, God comes close to us that we might see Him in a new way, a fuller way, to see His character more vividly and powerfully than ever before. It is a view we are at first hesitant to take as resentment over negative circumstances makes us want to turn away from Him. But an important part of our restoration, our growth and maturity in our faith, is the ability to see God's love and mercy in the midst of pain. It is easy to recognize His goodness in good times, but were that to remain our only perspective, it would make us, our faith, and even our worship weak and shallow. Remembering God's character, or maybe learning about it for the first time, is a critical part of our restoration, and perhaps the most difficult, but our restoration comes through gaining a clearer vision of God and His character.

THE TEMPTATION TO QUIT BELIEVING

Have you ever been through a time when everything in life just seems to have gone wrong? Maybe you're there right now. When that happens, it can be difficult to believe in the love and kindness of God. When bad things happen, especially if we feel we aren't deserving of them, it's easy to develop a cynicism, a hardness to those simple truths about God we have come to believe, cherish, and trust. The fact that God loves you and has a wonderful plan for your life doesn't seem to ring so true anymore.

In our cynicism, we are tempted to see such truths as relics of a gullible youth, dreamy-eyed optimism, or immaturity. We decide it's time to face life "realistically." Words about God's kindness and love and care for us begin to be difficult to hear, because too many circumstances in our life seem to challenge that idea. So we decide that it's time to quit believing in childhood relics like Santa Claus, the Easter bunny, the tooth fairy . . . the faithfulness of God, the protection of God, and even the compassion of God.

Remember how bitter Naomi had become over the death of her husband and two sons? She felt deserted, afflicted, and punished by God. She had developed a cynicism born of having one thing after another go bad in her life. She felt she had been cursed by God and was obviously beginning to have doubts about the love and kindness of God. How could God be loving and kind and then leave her destitute and lonely in her old age?

At the end of Ruth 1, Naomi was complaining bitterly about what God had done to her; how to her it seemed that He was intentionally and callously afflicting her. She even attempted to rename herself from Naomi (pleasant) to Mara (bitter). She didn't stop believing in God, but like C. S. Lewis, she began to entertain doubts about His character. This is something that virtually every believer will face at some point.

I remember a time when I had begun to develop a cynicism about the true nature and character of God. While I never doubted there was a God, I had begun to doubt what I had been told of Him. I was about sixteen years of age and had been a Christian for two years, having endured three broken homes by that time. Life was predictably difficult with the continual upheavals in our home. My mother, two sisters, and I were living in Palos Verdes, California, at the time, an affluent neighborhood. I couldn't help but notice that all my friends still had their biological mother and father in the home. They didn't have to deal with the pain I did, and couldn't really understand my pain since they didn't have anything to compare it to. My third father had left us in a home a single mother couldn't afford, and we lived on borrowed time.

While my friends were deciding what college they wanted to attend, I *dreamed* of what college I wanted to attend, and then I hunted like crazy for a school I could afford. At seventeen, I was working full-time, going to college full-time, and living alone in an apartment in a loud, cramped, and dangerous city, a far cry from the affluent surroundings I had been used to.

Many of my friends went away to college and its parties and sports. They had tuition paid through scholarships or parents, cars to drive, even spending allowances. While that was going on, I attended night school for three years to get my degree. My social life was nonexistent because of the time my minimum wage job and schooling took up. I began to feel *very* sorry for myself and recall how my entire life seemed to be uphill. All the cards seemed stacked against me. When I became a Christian, I expected a lot of that to change, and it didn't!

What was hardest was the fact that I was trying to enter the ministry, dedicating my entire life to serving God. I began to feel significantly put out that those who were only nominally committed to God had a seemingly easier life, yet I seemed to receive blow after blow. Cynicism began to creep in. God didn't have to roll out the red carpet for me, but He sure didn't have to make it so hard either, I thought.

Now, you have probably noticed what I came to understand later. My life wasn't horrible. Millions of people were a lot worse off than I was and had to deal with harder blows than I did, but I was comparing my plight with those of my peers, whose parents were wealthy, the 3 to 4 percent of America who is. God never promised I'd have no problems, or that He'd keep me in a certain socioeconomic lifestyle. I was simply feeling sorry for myself. Henry Ward Beecher wrote, "God's blessings steal into life noiselessly. They are neither self-proclaiming nor even self-announcing."[3] God's mercy and blessings surrounded me on every side, yet I was blind to them. They never shouted and grabbed my attention the way my difficulties did. And, frankly, self-pity is more enjoyable an exercise than faith.

It took a while for God to break through and prove to me the validity of the truths I had once believed about His character. I began to appraise them again, one by one, like lost heirlooms that helped recall fond memories of the God I had once known. I remembered the joy, freedom, and confidence these truths brought.

And that is what chapter 2 of the book of Ruth is about—Naomi reappraising the elements of God's character that she had cast aside as worthless. The dawn began to erase her darkness, and slowly what she had been blinded to became clear once again. Hannah Hurnard wrote, "If we try to resist loss and change or to hold on to blessings and joy belonging to a past which must drop away from us, we postpone all the new blessings awaiting us on a higher level and find ourselves left in a barren, bleak winter of sorrow and loneliness."[4]

Naomi walked close to the edge of despair in her assessment of God's character, but God stepped in and reminded Naomi of His true nature. We're going to see Naomi rediscover God's faithfulness, God's protection, and God's compassion.

GOD'S FAITHFULNESS

In *Quest for Character*, Chuck Swindoll recalls the true story of Jay Rathman, who was hunting deer in northern California. Rathman climbed a ledge on the slope of a rocky gorge, but as he raised his head to look over the ledge above, he sensed movement to the right of his face. A four-foot rattlesnake had struck at him, just missing his right ear.

The snake's fangs got snagged in the neck of Rathman's wool turtleneck sweater, and the force of the strike caused it to land on his left shoulder. The snake then coiled around his neck. He grabbed it behind the head with his left hand and could feel the warm venom running down the skin of his neck, the rattles making a furious racket. He fell backward and slid headfirst down the steep slope through brush and lava rocks, his rifle and binoculars bouncing beside him. "As luck would have it," he said in describing the incident to a department of Fish and Game official, "I ended up wedged between some rocks with my feet caught uphill from my head. I could barely move." He got his right hand on his rifle and used it to disengage the fangs from his sweater, but the snake had enough leverage to strike again. Rathman shared, "He made about eight attempts and managed to hit me with his nose just below my eye about four times. I kept my face turned so he couldn't get a good angle with his fangs, but it was very close. This chap and I were eyeball to eyeball and I found out that snakes don't blink. He had fangs like darning needles . . . I had to choke him to death. It was the only way out. I was afraid that with all the blood rushing to my head I might pass out." When he tried to toss the dead snake aside, he couldn't let go—"I had to pry my fingers from its neck." Rathman estimates his encounter with the snake lasted twenty minutes.[5]

Sometimes our experiences have a way, like that snake, of knocking us off balance and wrapping themselves around us. Just like the strike of the snake, these attacks cause us to reevaluate our level of protection, our sense of security in God. Naomi felt destitute of all the things that had previously brought her security and fulfillment. The strike that took her husband, the strike that took her first son, and finally the strike that took her last son caused her to seriously reevaluate God's faithfulness.

Dr. Jerome Frank talks about our "assumptive world." We all make assumptions about life, God, ourselves, others, and the way things are. He argues that "when our assumptions are true to reality, we live relatively happy, well-adjusted lives. But when our assumptions are distant from reality, we become confused and angry and disillusioned."[6]

In her limited perspective, Naomi couldn't imagine her security and fulfillment needs being met in any other way than through her husband and sons. She probably didn't see any way she could completely trust in God's faithfulness again. But God wanted to strengthen her understanding of His ability to provide for her in the midst of all situations.

I'm sure at this point in Naomi's life, it was difficult for her to trust God with her future with much confidence or hope. To experience security and fulfillment, we tell ourselves that we need a husband or wife, or children, or a good job, or a dazzling resume, or popularity, or health, or power, or the realization of our dearest ambitions and dreams—whatever it is that means security and fulfillment to us. For Naomi, it was through her husband and sons. It probably never occurred to her that God could meet her need in some other way.

Ruth 1 ended with Naomi bitter, hurting, and discouraged. Look how God starts Ruth 2: "Now Naomi had a kinsman of her husband, a man of great wealth, of the family of Elimelech, whose name was Boaz." Immediately after Naomi verbalized her distress at God's affliction and abandonment of her—His faithlessness in her eyes—God began to vindicate himself. Could God actually meet that need in some other way? Now look at verses 2–3:

> And Ruth the Moabitess said to Naomi, "Please let me go to the field and glean among the ears of grain after one in whose sight I may find favor." And she said to her, "Go, my daughter." So she departed and went and gleaned in the field after the reapers; and she happened to come to the portion of the field belonging to Boaz, who was of the family of Elimelech.

She just happened to. Coincidence? Could God actually meet Naomi's need for security and fulfillment through a Moabitess and a relative of Elimelech?

The faithfulness of God was circling and encompassing her, but she couldn't see it yet. These few verses form the basis of the method God was going to use to meet Naomi's need. God would meet Naomi's need not through a husband and sons, but through her daughter-in-law and a relative of her husband's. I wouldn't have wished anybody much luck if he or she had tried to convince Naomi of that before it happened, but that's how God was going to do it. And we learn such a valuable lesson from this story for our own lives.

God's provision doesn't always come in the forms we think or expect it should. It often comes from places we could never imagine, which is precisely the problem. Because we can't imagine something happening, we see no hope there.

We will see at the end of Ruth 2 that Naomi again rejoiced in God's faithfulness to her, that He had not forgotten about her or abandoned her. But first we have to deal with a similar aspect of God's care that Naomi obviously struggled with, which was God's protection.

GOD'S PROTECTION

After the death of her husband and sons, Naomi felt vulnerable, unprotected from life's disasters. She was no longer confident of the reality of God's protection in her life. After all, God had allowed the wolves to come right up to the front door; she probably had little confidence that He wouldn't also let them in.

One of the greatest fears in life is that feeling of being left vulnerable, unprotected, a victim of fate—that horrible feeling that you're surrounded and outnumbered by hostile forces and nobody is watching over your welfare. It can be overwhelming and spiritually disorienting.

Pastor and author Haddon Robinson shares a story about his father, who passed away at age eighty-eight:

> During his last adult years, my father lived with us in Texas. Before that he lived in New York City. His family lived in an area of New York called Harlem, in a section of Harlem called Mouse Town, a neighborhood that *Reader's Digest* said was the toughest section in the United States. The two years before my father came to live with us in

Dallas, he was beaten up twice by thugs. Once he was knocked down two flights of stairs and went to the hospital. The second time he was beaten up, he developed a hernia.

My father didn't know what the hernia was, and being a man of simple, perhaps even simplistic faith, he asked God to heal him. But nothing happened. When he finally wrote to me to tell me what had occurred, it was obvious that he was deeply upset. I received his letter in the morning, and by that afternoon I was on a plane to New York. A day or two later, I brought my father back to Texas, where the surgeons successfully operated on him.

My father felt that somehow God had let him down. He had prayed for healing, and the healing had not occurred. I tried to explain to my father that the hand of the physician was the hand of God, but he shrugged all of that off, and the last eight years of my father's life were not good ones. Not only were these years a time of declining health, but he went through them with a diminished faith.[7]

Such was the danger for Naomi, so it is with some wonder that we see in verses 4–16 a beautiful picture of God demonstrating his protection to a hurting and confused woman. Let's look at some of the examples of God's protection to her.

In verses 4–7 we read that Ruth, Naomi's link to life, was guided providentially to the field of Boaz, one of the few godly Jews in that dark period of Israel's history, one who not only observed the law of God, but the spirit of the law as well. What were the odds humanly that this would happen?

In verses 8–9 Boaz allowed Ruth to glean in his fields, which was her divine right, not simply an act of charity. Yet he goes beyond the law and concerns himself with her protection. Unscrupulous Hebrew farmers would find ways to keep gleaners out of their fields. Boaz goes beyond what was required and offers Ruth the protection of being among his maids, his own workers. Boaz knew she'd be safer in his fields than others. He also commanded his servants not to touch her. The line between where gleaners were and were not allowed to glean was not clearly marked, so when a gleaner would get too close to the wrong area, they would be beaten back. Boaz commanded his workers to leave Ruth alone. Furthermore, he offered her the water drawn for his workers. To get her own water in the middle of the day would have taken her a long time and diminished how much grain she could gather. Boaz was not under obligation to offer water, but he did. Again, we see in verses 10–13 an example of God's behind-the-scenes work in the community. Look at Ruth's question: "Why have I found favor in your sight that you should take notice of me, since I am a foreigner?" Boaz's answer was instructive: "All that you have done for your mother-in-law after the death of your husband has been fully reported to me, and how you left your father and your mother and the land of your birth, and came to a people that you did not previously know. May the LORD reward your work, and your wages be full from the LORD, the God of Israel, under whose wings you have come to seek refuge."[8] People were talking about Ruth's good character, which led Boaz to offer her physical protection. What if Boaz had *not* been told about Ruth's situation? God is working in the shadows of her life, invisible but powerful.

In these verses, we also see emotional encouragement. How Boaz's words must have brought comfort to Ruth, a stranger in a strange new land. They represent the first positive thing that has happened to her since entering the land of promise. Ruth was gleaning in a foreign land among people she did not know. She must have been nervous about the reception she was going to get being a Moabitess. Boaz was probably the only one in Israel who would have given her that kind of reception. Surely Ruth would pass along the emotional encouragement to Naomi.

Finally, in verses 14–16 we see Boaz providing food for Ruth normally reserved for himself and his workers. She didn't have to work on an empty stomach, and was able to take food home to Naomi as well. Furthermore, she is given a tremendous advantage with Boaz allowing her to glean near the reapers in order to get the most grain. Since being close to the reapers might leave her open to ridicule or mishandling by the workers, he instructs them to treat her with respect. Then he goes further and tells the reapers to leave some grain unbundled for her to pick up. Has God really abandoned Naomi? The evidence is in. Not only has He not abandoned Naomi, He has planned her deliverance long ago.

God protects Naomi through protecting Ruth. Far from being abandoned, Naomi was being lovingly protected from the myriad of dangers that could have imperiled her by the very God she had suspected of abandoning her.

GOD'S COMPASSION

It's obvious after reading Ruth 1 that Naomi felt punished and abandoned. She couldn't see any evidence of God's loving-kindness toward her. Because of circumstances she couldn't understand, she had lost confidence in God's compassion. She wasn't the first.

Job, whom God allowed Satan to afflict, lost all his wealth, all his children, and finally his health. His wife, seeing the calamity, could not acknowledge God anymore. Her words, as she saw him sitting in ashes, scraping his boils with a piece of broken pottery, dejected but still faithful to God, were, "Do you still hold fast your integrity? Curse God and die!" (Job 2:9). She had lost her belief in God's compassion. How could a compassionate God allow the righteous to suffer? Job's response was, "You speak as one of the foolish women speaks. Shall we indeed accept good from God and not accept adversity?" Philip Yancey writes,

> A friend of mine went swimming in a large lake at dusk. As he was paddling at a leisurely pace about a hundred yards offshore, a freak evening fog rolled in across the water. Suddenly he could see nothing: no horizon, no landmarks, no objects or lights on shore. Because the fog diffused all light, he could not even make out the direction of the setting sun. For thirty minutes he splashed around in panic. He would start off in one direction, lose confidence, and turn ninety degrees to the right. Or left—it made no difference which way he turned. He could feel his heart racing uncontrollably. He would stop and float, trying to conserve energy, and force himself to breathe slower. Then he would blindly strike out again. At last he heard a faint voice calling from shore. He pointed his body toward the sounds and followed them to safety. Something like that sensation of utter lostness must have settled in on Job as he sat in the rubble and tried to comprehend what had happened. He too had lost all landmarks, all points of orientation. Where should he turn? God, the one Person who could guide him through the fog, stayed silent. [9]

In fact, the whole point of the "wager" was to keep Job in the dark. "Does Job fear God for nothing?" Satan had asked. "Have You not made a hedge about him and his house and all that he has, on every side? You have blessed the work of his hands, and his possessions have increased in the land. But put forth Your hand now and touch all that he has; he will surely curse You to Your face" (Job 1:9–11). Anyone will trust in a God who spoils his favorite with great wealth. But remove all props, withdraw into the darkness, and then see what happens. The moment God accepted the terms of the wager, the fog rolled in around Job.

God ultimately "won the wager." Although Job questioned everything about God in a stream of angry outbursts and bitter complaints, and although he despaired of life and longed for death, he stubbornly refused to give up on God. Job defiantly maintained, "Though He slay me, I will hope in Him" (Job 13:15). He believed when there was no reason to believe, when nothing at all made sense. He believed in the middle of the fog.

Job stands as the most extreme example of what happens to be a universal law of faith. The kind of faith God wants seems to develop best when everything fuzzes over, when the lights get turned off, when the fog rolls in.[10] As Paul Tournier said, "Where there is no longer any opportunity for doubt, there is no longer any opportunity for faith either."[11]

In Naomi's life, the fog had been heavy and she had become spiritually disoriented. Then God stepped in.

> So she [Ruth] gleaned in the field until evening. Then she beat out what she had gleaned, and it was about an ephah of barley. She took it up and went into the city, and her mother-in-law saw what she had gleaned. She also took it out and gave Naomi what she had left after she was satisfied. Her mother-in-law then said to her, "Where did you glean today and where did you work? May he who took notice of you be blessed." So she told her mother-in-law with whom she had worked and said,

"The name of the man with whom I worked today
is Boaz." Naomi said to her daughter-in-law, "May
he be blessed of the LORD who has not withdrawn
his kindness to the living and to the dead." Again
Naomi said to her, "The man is our relative, he is
one of our closest relatives." (Ruth 2:17–20)

Notice two phrases that Naomi uses to describe Boaz: "May
he who took notice of you be blessed," and "May he be blessed of
the LORD who has not withdrawn his kindness to the living and to
the dead." Who had sent Boaz? Who had prepared all the parts of
the drama so that every character was in their proper place at precisely the right time? The very God she was convinced had removed
His compassion from her. Since God was behind Ruth coming into
contact with Boaz, God was really the one who had taken notice of
Ruth, and it was God who had not withdrawn His kindness to the
living and to the dead. The God of compassion had never stopped
being compassionate to Naomi; she just had not been able to see it
before this point. The fog is beginning to burn off. Naomi is beginning to realize that God's compassion never stops toward us. His
love for us isn't a fickle human love that can start and stop again, but
one that never ends or diminishes in fervency.

Many years ago, my son, Andrew, who was four at the time,
needed special discipline for an attitude problem he had. Children
go through phases where they test you to see if you'll remain consistent in your discipline before they give up the attitude. He'd tested
me all day and I had been consistent. That night, after his day of
continual discipline for the same thing, Andrew sat on the floor and
in a hurt and confused little voice asked, "Daddy, do you like me?"
How confused Andrew must have been. In his young mind the only
conclusion he could draw from my actions was that I didn't like
him anymore. I reached down and picked him up and said, "Yes,

Andrew, I love you very much. It's *because* I love you so much that I discipline you. I need to teach you to obey, because it's the only way I can keep you safe, and I love you too much to not want to keep you safe."

I empathize with his feelings. When things don't go my way or seem to go against me, I am often tempted to question the compassion of God, the extent of His love toward me, as if the real test of God's love was allowing me to get everything I want and have everything go my way. In looking back on my life, I can see clearly that it was the compassion and love of God that prompted Him not to give me the things I wanted and thought I needed.

In Ruth 2 we see Naomi beginning to reappraise the faithfulness, protection, and compassion of her God. She did not do it voluntarily, but as the evidence began to pile up, it became clear that God was watching over her.

ARE YOU SEARCHING FOR THE REAL GOD?

I have heard Christians share that while they have no problem with this or that aspect of God, there is one particular part of His nature or character they really struggle with. I know if I probe long enough I'll find the reason. Misinterpreting circumstances or just too deeply hurt to maintain perspective, we can be tempted to reduce our God, to denigrate Him to something other than He is. What's truly tragic is that doing that doesn't make us any happier; instead we become more miserable, hard, cynical, callous, and cold because the God we are left with after we have removed some of His essential characteristics isn't one we enjoy worshiping or long to love.

What aspect of God's character might you need to reappraise? His goodness? His kindness? His love? His holiness? His justice? His provision? His protection? If you remove just one of these characteristics from Him, He becomes an idol to you, something made by your own hands. You cannot remove one aspect of God's character and be left with the true God. They are all essential to His deity.

If you struggle with an aspect of God's character, I urge you to begin an investigation. You can't afford to let this issue slide. God said, "You shall have no other gods before Me. You shall not make for yourself an idol" (Exodus 20:3–4). An idol is simply our attempt to reduce or design God to fit our current understanding of Him.

Years ago I was in an antique shop and a friend pointed out an interesting object for sale. A small box had a sign next to it that read, "7 gods for ½ off!" Sometime in the past, someone who believed in these gods had lost confidence in them and discarded them. While these weren't true gods, the same danger lurks in each of our lives, that we might lose confidence in our God and eventually discard our faith in His marvelous character and nature.

In Sheldon Vanauken's book *A Severe Mercy*, he tells of the overwhelming grief he suffered after the death of his wife, Davy. He felt completely alone, without the comfort of God or people. One night as he lie awake, he decided to reject God, to turn his back on his faith. But no matter how much he tried to reject God, no matter how much he tried to deny God's existence, he found that he just couldn't do it. His faith was so ingrained in his heart and mind and spirit, so much a part of his every fiber, that it didn't do any good to deny it. He simply couldn't reject God.[12]

If you realize that you might have lost confidence in some part of God's nature or character, trace your steps and look at it objectively. What led you to question God's character? What event planted the doubt? It's so easy to allow a seed of doubt to take root in your mind about an aspect of God's character. That's one of Satan's methods for deceiving Christians. He tried it with Job, and he'll try it with you. Guaranteed. If you are still struggling after you've traced the idea's origin, ask a mature Christian to help you. Ask God to help you understand Him more clearly—He delights to answer that prayer.

If you have lost faith in an aspect of God's character, begin to reappraise it.

To be restored means you will see God again as He really is, not as circumstances would seem to dictate. What was lost needs to be found. What was twisted needs to be straightened. What was broken needs to be repaired.

What was forgotten needs to be remembered.

CHAPTER 6

Naomi's Transformed Desires

One's philosophy is not best expressed in words;
it is expressed in the choices one makes . . . In
the long run, we shape our lives and we shape
ourselves. The process never ends until we die.
And the choices we make are ultimately our
responsibility.

Eleanor Roosevelt (1884–1962)

THESE DAYS MOST PEOPLE TAKE PICTURES ON digital cameras. In a matter of minutes, images download from the camera to a computer. Some people, however, prefer to use film cameras and develop the photographs themselves. Film is developed in a darkroom where light cannot destroy the picture, and the process takes time. The photographer must work in the dark and patiently wait for a photograph to completely develop.

In a way, this is the process God uses to transform our character. He takes us into a "darkroom" or difficult time in our lives and works to develop something beautiful in us. However, sometimes the beautiful picture He seeks to develop is quite a different picture than the one we have in mind. Most of us have the American ideal as the desire of our hearts—to be attractive, desired, powerful, rich, and famous.

Gordon MacDonald, in his book, *Living at High Noon*, recounts the experience of sitting next to a well-known television star on a transatlantic flight:

> For almost five hours we talked about some of the salient issues of life. My traveling partner had no hesitation in admitting he was a bored, unhappy man, feeling betrayed that success had brought him so little of that feeling of excitement he'd expected when he'd started. Looking back on our conversation, I now realize that at mid-life he was still tyrannized by the thought that, given enough success, his job would become one long orgy of excitement and satisfaction. I remember saying to him, "You know, you already have the three things the average American male thinks epitomizes vocational success: a beautiful young wife, more money from your work than you could ever spend, and a name so popular that in two lifetimes you can't handle all the invitations you get." The memory of what my friend said on the plane has stuck with me. "You're right; I've got all that. But it's those very things that have conspired to make me generally miserable. For you see now that I have achieved them, I know—unlike those still reaching for them—that they're not worth having, not worth working as hard for as I've done."[1]

Here is someone who has everything a normal person would want, and yet he admits that he is "generally miserable." Even so, if you ask most people if getting everything they desire in life would make them happy, most would say yes. Enthusiastically!

We're going to see in this chapter how desires are the battleground for our souls. They are where God develops character. A mentor of mine, Wally Norling, once told me, "The secret to success in life is learning to love the right things." So much of our unhappiness and discontent is connected with desiring the *wrong things*. In His restoration of us, God wants to reset our default setting—to return us to seeking first His kingdom and His righteousness (see Matthew 6:33). In restoring us, God wants to transform our desires.

For most of us, it's not an easy sell.

TRANSFORMING OUR DESIRES

As God is restoring your life, He will begin first in your heart. Restoration begins from the inside out, and that transformation is God's will for us in Christ (see Romans 12:1–2).

If desires are the battleground for our souls, then what side was winning in Naomi's life? What desires did God need to transform in her? As we look at Naomi's story, we can see some desires that led to a confused understanding of God's will in her life. We've looked at some of these issues in light of what distress revealed in Naomi's character, but now we see how Naomi's transformed desires contributed to her restoration.

First, she desired to experience only good things from God. This might seem like the most normal of desires—after all, who says, "I'd like to experience bad things from God?" When she called herself Mara or "bitter," she was making a statement about her experience with God and life. From her perspective, she hadn't received good things, only things that caused her to be bitter. She had a bad taste in her mouth about God and the life He had chosen for her. Yet, it would be these very "bad things" that God would use to guide Naomi into amazing blessings in her future.

The problem is that good things, when they aren't balanced with difficulties, don't tend to create character, or at least the right kind. I have had the privilege of knowing several people who have had everything this world can offer, much like the famous actor. I've also talked with them after they've lost it all.

All.

Yet, though the process was painful, these people speak with uncommon faith and wisdom, and have characters refined through difficulties. All the things they desired (and got) conspired to make them shallow, proud, self-centered, and arrogant. The loss of the "good things" brought a wonderful perspective on what is important and what isn't. They started learning to love the right things—and it paid dividends in their life.

Desserts are wonderful, but a steady diet of them leads to malnutrition and serious illness. God needed to transform the character of Naomi into a godly one, and having more of the "good life" wasn't going to make it happen.

Second, Naomi desired to find her security in her husband and sons. Every Hebrew woman desired a husband, sons, and God willing, many grandchildren! It is completely understandable that Naomi put her security in what made her *feel* secure. But when her husband died, and then her sons, the foundation she was standing on crumbled. It was not wrong for her to desire a husband and children; the danger was in finding her security in those relationships. A seemingly normal desire can often keep us from trusting our security to God and His will.

When those things she placed her security in were removed, she was understandably crushed, but more importantly, it appears she was convinced that security was unobtainable because the method she trusted in had failed her. She had lost any hope of security. Yet, she was going to discover that God would provide all she needed for her future and happiness.

Before she realized she could depend on God, her frustration led to the next desire that God needed to transform, a desire to withdraw when pain hit. The pain she felt from the loss of her husband and sons, and the shame she probably felt as a less than "pleasant" Hebrew woman, conspired to create within her a desire to escape and withdraw. When her daughters-in-law tried to stay with her and join her in her pain, she tried to get them to leave her alone. Yet, God was going to bless her through the very people she was pushing away. If she had gotten her way, she would have isolated herself from everyone God sent to help her. A feeling of shame can separate us from those God has sent to minister His grace and love to us.

Additionally, Naomi desired to define God's work and character by how she felt about Him at the moment. Naomi was obviously disenchanted with God's work in her life, and her statement to the women of Bethlehem left no doubt that she saw God as the one responsible for her pain. She wanted to define all of God's work in her life, and His character, by how she felt about Him at the moment. That's very tempting. When we know God is sovereign and what He wills occurs, it can be hard not to feel put out when it appears He has chosen painful situations for us to endure. It becomes tempting to define God as an uncaring, unloving, distant, or uninvolved God because He has allowed something bad to happen in my life. We no longer look to understand His character through the Scriptures, or by recalling His past mercies to us, but instead we view Him through the lens of our latest difficulty. Surely Naomi wanted her life to be the "ideal" life. She wanted the perfect tent with the white picket fence outside (in those days, people lived in tents). She wanted to grow old with Elimelech in a fertile and peaceful Israel, surrounded by her two strong sons and their *Jewish* wives. She wanted the life without the pain, without the loss, without the tests of faith, without the questions.

Frankly, so do I. Some people seem to get that life. They have everything *we* most fervently desire. The ironic reality is that while they are living *our* most desired life, frequently they aren't living *their* most desired life (see our friend the actor).

Have you noticed that desire in life is like our appetite for food? Our appetite can only be satisfied for a while before it wants something else, something more. This is why our desires so often feed our discontent—our desires are insatiable. It is here, therefore, that God must do an important work. Not all our desires are worthwhile—despite how much we desire them.

There are few more painful processes in life than the one in which we are forced to reexamine our dearest desires, and to finally, with great pain and tears of anguish, let them go. But this process allows us to be open to the avenue God has chosen to bless us in.

Think of what desires Naomi had to surrender to God: a long life with her husband in the place of her choice; healthy, happy sons as long as she lived; a life surrounded by familiarity and financial security; and a faith in God that would never need to be tested.

To allow God to transform us, we need to be able to admit to ourselves that God made us, and only He knows what would bring about our transformation to joy, spiritual health, and purpose. We tend to fight God's methods, because, frankly, we've grown rather attached to our own desires. Through restoration, God wants to make us better than the sum of our insatiable or misdirected desires—He wants to make us godly. He wants our character to display real trust, real kindness, real righteousness, and real selflessness.

GUARDING AGAINST SHORTCUTS

When we want something badly, it is difficult to be patient for it. We are reluctant to take the chance that we might "miss out," and it becomes tempting to take shortcuts to assure that what we want to happen truly happens. How many times have you or I seen a Christian desperately chasing a certain desire? Whether it is a young person seeking to find a boyfriend or girlfriend, or a single man or woman wanting to get married, or a person wanting to get ahead in their vocation, the issue can become an intense desire that affects all one does. That desire, if it is not checked by a strong trust in God's sovereignty (the belief that He sees your need and will act accordingly) can lead to dangerous shortcuts.

Often the first opportunity that comes to people seeking after their desires isn't a godly one at all. But in the rush to have the need met, they ignore the fact that what they perceive to be the answer to their prayer is in reality a temptation to compromise and sin. Consider the following quote:

> I would like to reach out to all the people who have hurt like I have hurt, and searched like I have searched and are close to giving up hope. I would like to tell them that there's always a way out. Just when you think your story is over, there's a miracle around the corner. Don't give up hope. Just look up—that's where your source is, where to find your strength.

These words sound so encouraging, so inspiring, so trusting of God. But let's put them in their proper context. In the 1980s, a famous televangelist, Jim Bakker, was caught in a sexual sin with a woman named Jessica Hahn. She claimed that the scandal had brought her to the brink of suicide on her twenty-eighth birthday, and she prayed to God for a miracle. "The next day," Jessica recalled, "*Playboy* called. That was my miracle." She claimed the nude photo layout and her interview helped her restore her sense of self-worth and brought her closer to God. She went on to explain, "I have a plaque in my room here at the Playboy Mansion that reads, 'JESSICA, TRUST ME. I

HAVE EVERYTHING UNDER CONTROL. SIGNED, JESUS.'
What the future is, I know it will be part of His plan."[2]

The scandal revealed clearly that neither Jessica Hahn nor Jim Bakker displayed true Christian characteristics. Was the call from *Playboy* truly the leading of God? Is a nude layout in a pornographic magazine a way to restore a godly sense of self-worth? Does God rescue us by leading us to sin? A deep and passionate desire for celebrity and notoriety combined with a tragic misunderstanding of God's character led Jessica Hahn to believe that posing nude and the resulting celebrity were God's will for her life. She was deceived. She wasn't the first, and she won't be the last.

It is easy to spout words of trust and love of God, until we are faced with trusting God and choosing obedience to Him over our dearest earthly desires. C. S. Lewis, writing of the struggle he encountered with God over the loss of his beloved wife, Joy, wrote,

> Bridge players tell me that there must be some money on the game "or else people won't take it seriously." Apparently it's like that. Your bid—for God or no God, for a good God or the Cosmic Sadist, for eternal life or nonentity—will not be serious if nothing much is staked on it. And you will never discover how serious it was until the stakes are raised horribly high, until you find that you are playing not for counters or for sixpences but for every penny you have in the world.[3]

DEVELOPING CHARACTER THROUGH RELEASING OUR DESIRES

Naomi could have allowed her bitterness and confusion to blind her to God's character and moving. This resistance could have sabotaged her faith and changed her responses to the events that would become significant.

Would she have been spiritually alert enough to sense God's hand in Boaz's activities had she insisted on clinging to her bitterness? Might she not have just "checked out" and ignored or downplayed Ruth's news? At some point, Naomi had to release her desires to God. She had to surrender.

So will we.

Transformed desires are the way God chooses to transform our character and our faith. It seems strange to think that some desires that we hold most dear—that we have convinced ourselves we could never be happy unless they were completely fulfilled—might be the very things holding back the full blessing God has for us.

The blessings come in two ways. First, they come in the peace of heart and mind that comes from finally surrendering your desires to God's will. Unfulfilled desires are often the most significant issue keeping us from a closer walk with God and a deeper trust in Him. It isn't that what you desire is necessarily wrong—the desires that Naomi surely had weren't wrong—they just weren't God's plan for her. In the same way, our desires may not be wrong either. A desire to be married, healthy, financially comfortable; a desire to have children or a certain job, to live in a certain place, to attain a certain goal—these desires aren't wrong or sinful, which is why it seems so clear to us that God would want to fulfill our desires. Yet, God often chooses to meet the needs these desires reveal in us in a different way. And that isn't negotiable. When we finally cease resisting His will, we find peace through surrender.

The second way God blesses us through transforming our desires is that we finally become receptive to the way God *does* intend on blessing us. We become willing to accept an idea or plan we hadn't considered before. There we find God's blessing. It looks different than we had imagined—but we find that it is, indeed, good. And in the process *we* are changed along with our desires. Our faith matures, our openness to God's will grows, our belief that we know what is best finally quiets. It is difficult to get to this place, but wonderful to arrive.

Archbishop Fulton Sheen said, "Self-discipline never means giving up anything, for giving up is a loss. Our Lord did not ask us to give up the things of earth, but to exchange them for better things." What might God be asking us to give up in order to receive *better* things, and, more importantly, to become more Christlike in the process?

WHAT DO YOU LOVE?

Lillian Doerksen spent fifty years of her life ministering in India. It wasn't the life she had envisioned for herself. When she was a student at Biola University (a Christian university in Southern California), she studied Christian education and, after graduation, planned to marry her handsome Royal Canadian airman boyfriend, Lloyd James. But then she felt God calling her to minister to orphans in India. She made the most difficult decision of her life. After praying that God would bring Lloyd a better wife than she ever could have been, she bid him farewell and left for India. At a Christian orphanage, she spent the next thirty-six years raising thirty-four girls she adopted. Later, after "retiring," she felt called to launch a ministry for the deaf as a result of her experience with her daughter's two deaf children. The state of Maharashtra, with a population of 90 million people, had no schools for the deaf. At the age of sixty-six, she founded the school, which now has camps, vocational training, weekly Bible fellowships, and a hostel to educate young girls. As she reflected back on her fifty years of ministry, she said, "It's been a very, very worthwhile life." What happened to her potential husband, Lloyd James? He married a wonderful Christian woman who became one of Lillian's closest friends.[4]

Lillian had her own desires to give up, didn't she? None of those desires were wrong—they just didn't reflect God's best for Lillian, and they didn't factor in all the people whose lives she would touch so deeply. What was the result of allowing God to transform her desires? "A very, very worthwhile life." How many of us can say the same?

I can't help comparing Lillian's experience with Gordon MacDonald's seatmate, the actor, who had everything our world says you need to be happy. Lillian had none of these things, yet she experienced more joy and happiness than the famous actor ever could.

Are you frustrated because your deepest and most intense desires aren't being realized? It is, of course, possible that God intends to fulfill those desires in His timing. On the other hand, you may be hanging on to desires that God wants you to relinquish. You won't know His plans for you until you are willing to surrender your desires to Him.

It is the *willingness* to relinquish the desires that is transformative. We become like our Lord, who dreaded the coming crucifixion and the cross, yet prayed to His heavenly Father in the Garden of Gethsemane, "Not as I will, but as You will" (Matthew 26:39). We enter a place of peace because we have relinquished our desires; God will be our hope and happiness, not the fulfillment of our desires.

The secret to life is learning to love the right things.

What do you love?

CHAPTER 7

Boaz's Authentic Character

Be kind; everyone you meet is fighting a hard battle.

Ian Maclaren (1850–1907)

WE CALL HIM THE FATHER OF OUR NATION, AND with good cause. General George Washington epitomized the American Revolution. His decisions and practical wisdom carried his troops and our fledgling republic to eventual victory. But it was not an easy road.

For eight long years Washington led his ragtag army through the rigors of war. His under-funded and under-supplied civilian army was prone to go home when the crops needed planting or harvesting. General Washington lost more battles than he won, and always avoided the direct head-to-head battle with the British he knew he would lose.

His character, however, was shown not mainly on the battlefield, but in his decisions when tempted with power. Twice during the revolution, in 1776 and again in 1777 when British advances forced the Congress to abandon Philadelphia, Washington was granted virtually dictatorial powers to maintain the army and the government. Both times Washington relinquished the power as soon as possible.

Several months after the final victory at Yorktown, a number of his disgruntled officers approached him. Frustrated with the Continental Congress and their slowness in keeping their promises to the soldiers, the officers suggested that America should establish a monarchy, and Washington should be its first king. They assured him they would support him. In response, Washington made a moving and emotional speech to his officers to rally them again to the ideals of the revolution for which they had fought.[1]

Then, after two terms in office as our first president, Washington refused to serve another term, though the office had no term limitations at that point. He could have, like Napoleon in France, consolidated his power and refused to relinquish it, but he didn't.[2] Instead, he retired to his plantation. An amazed King George III of England responded to this act by calling Washington "the greatest character of his age."

It wasn't until Washington was tempted to betray the ideals of the American Revolution by failing to relinquish power or refusing power that we could see his true character. In those pivotal moments, George Washington's authenticity was confirmed. He was, as so few really are, as advertised!

Sudden, decisive moments in our lives become our measures of authenticity. In those moments, a decision or action exposes the foundation we have built our lives on. That moment does not make us great or noble, or weak and compromising; it simply confirms what we have become. And what we are becoming has to do with the choices we make every day. C. S. Lewis in *Mere Christianity* writes, "Every time you make a choice you are turning the central part of you, the part that chooses, into something a little different than it was before. And taking your life as a whole, with all your innumerable choices, you are slowly turning this central thing either into a Heavenly creature or into a hellish creature."[3]

As we look at Ruth 3 and 4, we are going to see the character of Boaz in vivid detail, and we are going to ask ourselves the natural question: What characteristics had Boaz invested that made him a man of excellence? Boaz had taken the time to cultivate and nourish kindness, righteousness, and selflessness, and he practiced these character traits until they became natural for him.

KINDNESS

Henry Drummond said, "The greatest thing a man can do for his heavenly Father is to be kind to some of his other children."[4] Kindness is being sympathetic and patient with others.

We see Boaz's kindness first in Ruth 2. When Ruth came to his field to glean, and he noticed her, he immediately responded in kindness. He protected her in his fields and made sure she gleaned more than enough to feed her and her mother-in-law. He assured her that if she stayed in his fields, she would remain safe and well provided for. Ruth expressed surprise at the acts of Boaz: "I have found favor in your sight, my lord, for you have comforted me and indeed have spoken kindly to your maidservant, though I am not like one of your maidservants" (2:13). I find it interesting that the first thing that Boaz commented on about Ruth was her kindness to Naomi, and the first thing Ruth commented on about Boaz was his kindness to her. Coincidence? Hardly! We see how much Boaz and Ruth were made and meant for each other.

Had it not been for Boaz's kindness, Ruth and Boaz likely would not have married. It was Boaz's initial kindness—a character trait that he had nurtured before he ever met Ruth—that kept Ruth in his field instead of her going on to another. It was his kindness that comforted Ruth and prompted her to tell Naomi what had been done for her. In response to his kindness, Naomi had Ruth ask Boaz to marry her and fulfill the role of the kinsman redeemer.

Kindness. God can use it to accomplish so much in our lives, can't He? Sadly, we don't usually appreciate the wisdom of God when He calls us to practice a godly virtue like kindness—not understanding that He frequently chooses to bless our lives through this very characteristic and others. Neglecting these vital characteristics crimps the flow of God's blessings. Traits like honesty and holiness, cultivated and nurtured, will one day be a conduit of His special blessings in our life. When we neglect opportunities to develop these traits, we cut ourselves off from the blessings God would otherwise bestow upon us. How many of God's blessings in our lives have launched from godly characteristics like kindness?

Have you considered that God *created* us to be kind? Years ago a friend of mine, who ministers to American servicemen and women around the world, wrote in his newsletter about two sailors from a U.S. aircraft carrier that sailed into Phattaya, Thailand, for a port visit. This visit is a favorite port of many sailors because of the thousands of young women who work in the a-go-gos or prostitute bars for very little money. One sailor, however, was a Christian.

He was walking the streets with a friend trying to find something wholesome to do. In the process of doing this, he met a young prostitute. She seemed nice—not at all what the young man had expected. As they talked, this sailor made a decision: he invited the girl to spend the afternoon with himself and his friend. He made it clear he wanted nothing from her; on the contrary, he wanted her to just have a nice day. They spent the day walking along the ocean, talking, eating at a restaurant, and becoming friends. The sailor's motivation was simply kindness. The next day the carrier sailed off.

Some time later the carrier returned to Phattaya, and this sailor and his friend decided to try to find the same girl. When they found her, they paid the necessary money to "rent" her for the day and set off together with the simple intent of treating the girl like a person instead of an object. She had a nice, relaxing day apart from her "work."

During the next two days in port, while the sailor was on duty on the ship, he prayed about how he could help this young girl even more.

Later he and another sailor set out to find a church, but instead found a ministry that reached out to prostitutes to get them off the streets and into the kingdom of God. The young girl agreed to go to the mission and had a long talk with one of the counselors there. They learned that she was the oldest sister, and it was her job to sacrifice her life to make money for her family so that none of her sisters would have to do what she did. As the counselor shared the grace of Jesus with this young girl, she gave her heart to Christ. The two sailors then promised to help support this girl financially until she could get a new job and a new start in life.

Radical? Maybe, but somehow I can see our Lord Jesus doing this, can't you? In God's eternal plan, it was always His will that we would be kind in heart, for by displaying that characteristic we are mimicking Him and fulfilling His original intention for us. True kindness is so rare and so difficult to maintain in a world full of selfish, impatient, and unsympathetic people that it can only be found in those who truly seek it. It is all the more difficult to be kind because that characteristic can be a target for others who take advantage of that wonderful quality. However, true kindness is a rare virtue that will not be detoured by those who would test it severely.

Surely some of those who experienced Boaz's kindness in the past had taken advantage of it. His generous spirit, his tender sympathies, had surely been abused over the years—yet he refused to let those negative experiences alter his character. He was an older man now, experienced and tested in many ways, and yet his patient, sympathetic nature remained. Is it any wonder God was able to bring such great blessings to his life? His character, developed over time and with effort, allowed God to use Him and bless Him.

Anything we don't practice often enough seems awkward to us. If we have always protected ourselves from possible betrayal by rationing our kindness, it is we who have suffered, not those who would have abused our kindness. Our Lord's kindness is constantly betrayed and abused, yet He does not stop being kind, for it is in His nature. Indeed, as the Scriptures remind us, had He resolved to ration His kindness, we would never have been led to repentance or salvation (see Romans 2:4). Further, Paul tells us to be kind, tender-hearted, forgiving one another (Ephesians 4:32).

Boaz had invested in the characteristic of kindness; it was not awkward on him, and it fit him well. He didn't have to force it, it had become natural. He was kind. However, kindness is only one of the characteristics he had invested in. Another was righteousness.

RIGHTEOUSNESS

Righteousness is "being just, honorable, and free from guilt."[5] Righteousness has to do with your motivation, the *why* behind the *what*. It is clear that Boaz was concerned with being righteous. It is also clear that a significant motivation for both Boaz and Ruth in this whole event was observing the law of redemption, that of the kinsman redeemer, and all that it implied. Ruth wanted to continue the name of her husband, Mahlon, or even Naomi's husband, Elimelech.

It was upon this aspect of Boaz's character, his righteousness, that Naomi was counting when she sent Ruth to him in the middle of the night. We're not completely sure why she had Ruth go at night, but it might have been to give Boaz the chance to say no without an audience to witness it. No one would ever know if he simply rejected the offer. This speaks well of Naomi's wisdom and righteousness herself. She wasn't willing to put Ruth in a risky moral situation with Boaz, or a situation that could lead to damaged reputations. If this quality of righteousness had never been cultivated and evidenced in the life of Boaz, would Naomi have taken this chance? If Ruth had not been able to perceive a genuine righteousness in

Boaz's life, would she have been so willing to follow Naomi's rather unorthodox request?

Let's follow the account and see if we can bring enlightenment on what must appear a little strange. We must not try to understand this event with twenty-first century morals and customs. Naomi says to Ruth,

> "Behold, he winnows barley at the threshing floor tonight. Wash yourself therefore, and anoint yourself and put on your best clothes, and go down to the threshing floor; but do not make yourself known to the man until he has finished eating and drinking. It shall be when he lies down, that you shall notice the place where he lies, and you shall go and uncover his feet and lie down; then he will tell you what you shall do."
>
> She said to her, "All that you say I will do." So she went down to the threshing floor and did according to all that her mother-in-law had commanded her.
>
> When Boaz had eaten and drunk and his heart was merry, he went to lie down at the end of the heap of grain; and she came secretly, and uncovered his feet and lay down. It happened in the middle of the night that the man was startled and bent forward; and behold, a woman was lying at his feet. He said, "Who are you?" And she answered, "I am Ruth your maid. So spread your covering over your maid, for you are a close relative." Then he said, "May you be blessed of the LORD, my daughter. You have shown your last kindness to be better than the first by not going after young men, whether poor

or rich. Now, my daughter, do not fear. I will do for you whatever you ask, for all my people in the city know that you are a woman of excellence. Now it is true I am a close relative; however, there is a relative closer than I. Remain this night, and when morning comes, if he will redeem you, good; let him redeem you. But if he does not wish to redeem you, then I will redeem you, as the LORD lives. Lie down until morning."

So she lay at his feet until morning and rose before one could recognize another; and he said, "Let it not be known that the woman came to the threshing floor." Again he said, "Give me the cloak that is on you and hold it." So she held it, and he measured six measures of barley and laid it on her. (Ruth 3:2–15)

By the way, for any young woman reading this and searching for the man God would have you marry, this is not a prescription for finding a mate today. This situation was in complete accordance with ancient Semitic culture. In other words, don't try this at home! Try this in our culture and you'll find yourself in big trouble fast! Naomi was not asking Ruth to romantically entice Boaz with the hope that he would then want to marry her. That would have been deceitful, manipulative, and in every way counter to a real trust in God to meet their need in a holy and righteous manner. Remember, Ruth wasn't desperate to marry or she could have remained in Moab where her prospects were much better. Everything that occurred here was aboveboard, moral, and even customary. Ruth was asking Boaz to fulfill his responsibility to provide a name for his kinsman's offspring so that his kinsman's name would not disappear from Israel. That's precisely the way Boaz received it.

After Boaz fell asleep, Ruth uncovered his feet and slept cross-way at his feet under his covering. She was fully clothed, as was he. (The translation in verse 3 that reads "put on your best clothes" is an unfortunate rendering. Ruth was likely wearing a large, heavy cloth called a mantle. This mantle would cover her entirely, revealing only one eye. It would be virtually impossible to tell her apart from other maids dressed in this way, which is probably why Boaz didn't recognize her at dinner.) In verse 8 we read that Boaz woke up and saw that someone was sleeping at his feet. Naturally, he was startled.

When Ruth made her request, Boaz immediately understood what she was requesting.[6] Being a righteous man, Boaz understood her motivations. His character enabled him to see clearly. He didn't start looking at himself in the mirror and telling himself how well-preserved he was for a man his age, or how he always knew he was irresistible to women. He understood what was happening here and what Ruth and Naomi were seeking from him.

Boaz then showed concern for Ruth's reputation and the rights of the nearer kinsman by not letting anyone know she had come to him in the night. The nearer kinsman might want to redeem the land and marry her. Boaz's care of Ruth's reputation demanded that he deliver her with her unblemished reputation completely intact. The nearer kinsman would be able to fulfill the obligation with no misgivings. Boaz would not try, nor allow carelessness on his part, to sabotage the nearer kinsman's opportunity.

In this instance Boaz reminds me of Joseph, the husband of Mary, who had the opportunity to ruin Mary's reputation when she was found with child before he had experienced sexual relations with her, but he didn't take it. He desired to keep it quiet so as not to heap unnecessary shame on her. That distressing experience for Joseph revealed his character, and this event revealed Boaz's character. His righteousness wasn't fake, but real, substantial, genuine. He responded righteously in this situation because he had cultivated righteousness in every area of his life. He responded as had become his habit, and because of that God is able to bless him.

There is one more characteristic to mention, one that Ruth and Boaz shared and one that this story hinges on, and that is the characteristic of selflessness.

SELFLESSNESS

We need to remember that a child born of Ruth by Boaz as the kinsman redeemer would provide a son to carry on Mahlon's, or even Elimelech's, name, not Boaz's name. That your name would be carried on to posterity was of incredible importance in that day, and looking at the situation from a strictly human perspective, there was no real benefit to Boaz here. He didn't need Ruth: he was successful, had a great reputation, and was financially well off. Ruth and Naomi brought nothing to Boaz; in fact, they would financially diminish him because he would need to feed two more mouths, as well as any children the union with Ruth created. There was no social safety net in those days, so Boaz would have to take on *all* the needs of a number of people. What if there was another famine in the land with all these new mouths to feed?

It was no small thing that Boaz was willing to do, and only a truly selfless man would have even considered it. This is where Boaz's authentic selflessness is revealed. You don't just wake up one day and in a critical and decisive moment and act selflessly. You act selflessly because it has become your habit, because it is a part of your character.

Our culture makes selflessness difficult because it teaches us not to do anything that doesn't bring a payoff. In contrast, the selfless person assumes that there won't necessarily be one in this life. Selflessness that seeks a reward ceases to be selflessness. John Powell writes, "I doubt that there has ever been one recorded case of deep and lasting fulfillment reported by a person whose basic mind-set and only question was: What am I getting out of this?"[7] While God is able to bless in a myriad of ways, as we see with Boaz, the only guaranteed blessing is the understanding that you are acting as you should, and that God is pleased.

AUTHENTIC CHARACTER LIVED OUT

There are moments in our lives that define us, events that are designed to reveal what we are truly made of. In the book of Esther it was when she was willing to lose all she had gained in becoming Queen of Persia to say, "Thus will I go into the King, which is not according to the law; and if I perish, I perish" (Esther 4:16). With Daniel's three friends, it was their unwillingness to worship any other god but the true God, even if it meant being thrown into a furnace (Daniel 3). For Daniel himself, it meant continuing to pray every day to his God even when it meant he would be thrown into a den of ravenous lions (Daniel 6). With the disciples in the New Testament, it meant preaching Christ even under threat of persecution (Acts 4:13–22). With the apostle Paul, it meant accepting the loss of all his worldly credentials in order to gain Christ (Philippians 3:7–16).

You and I will have such moments as well, moments when events will reveal our true character and our true commitment to our God. I firmly believe that we need to have a moment of testing and faithfulness that we can look back on with satisfaction and say, "Yes, that cost me, but it was right. I did it because it was right, not because it was financially sound, or would create a better situation for me, but just because it was the right thing to do!"

These moments aren't accidents, and you can't prepare for them—at least, not specifically. You train for these great moments in all the thousands of little moments in which you seek to be kind, righteous, and selfless. You train for selfless moments by a selfless lifestyle. If you do this, you will find yourself in those great moments doing great things. It will have become your habit.

The truth is, *unless you live extraordinarily behind the scenes, you will never act extraordinarily when you are finally and unexpectedly thrust into the spotlight.* So many people dream of someday doing some great and selfless act that everyone will remember them for. But they never rehearse that dream in their everyday lives.

Boaz rehearsed for his moment. He developed kind, righteous, and selfless qualities that led him to make a decision that put him in the lineage of Jesus Christ. In the final chapter of Ruth, we see the climax of the story. Let's compare the attitudes and actions of the nearer kinsman and Boaz to see how Boaz lived out the authentic character he had developed.

In Ruth 4, Boaz went to the gate of the city. This is where locals gathered to deal with legal business transactions and public issues. Boaz waited until he saw the nearer kinsman, and then asked him to sit down. Then Boaz called for ten elders, which would make the proceeding legal. Everyone would surmise by this point that something important was going to occur.

Boaz informed the nearer kinsman, in the presence of all, how Naomi, who had gone to Moab and returned a widow, needed to sell her land, land that had originally been her husband Elimelech's.[8] Boaz pointed out that the right to redeem the land fell to the nearer kinsman. He also hastened to add that he, Boaz, was willing to redeem the land if the nearer kinsman was not willing.

This must have been a difficult time for Boaz, even though he was clearly a man who trusted God. He was more than willing to marry Ruth and fulfill his responsibility, both out of his regard for the law, Naomi's situation, and Ruth, yet the nearer kinsman had to be unwilling to fulfill his responsibility for Boaz to get his chance.

In verse 4 Boaz used an emphatic in the Hebrew language. When Boaz said, "If you will redeem it, redeem it; but if not, tell me that I may know; for there is no one but you to redeem it, and I am after you," the *I* was emphatic. Boaz was communicating his great interest in this project. But the nearer kinsman replied with an equally emphatic *I*: "*I, I* will redeem it."

Boaz said, I am *willing* to do it, and the nearer kinsman replied, I am *going* to do it! Up to this point, the nearer kinsman thought he was simply redeeming Naomi's land. Land meant more crops, more income, and a higher status. He probably thought that Boaz was after the same thing, and he wanted to make it clear that he wasn't going to pass on a great deal.

However, Boaz desired a different privilege. Boaz was already known as a great landowner, a wealthy and mighty man. It doesn't appear that the land acquisition held the same appeal to him. He wanted the privilege of marrying Ruth and assisting her in her effort to honor her husband and father-in-law by continuing their names through a son. Further, he probably wanted that privilege as badly as that nearer kinsman wanted the land.

In verse 5 Boaz told the kinsman redeemer, "On the day you buy the field from the hand of Naomi, you must also acquire Ruth the Moabitess, the widow of the deceased, in order to raise up the name of the deceased on his inheritance." At this news, the nearer kinsman made an about-face. He said, "I cannot redeem it for myself, because I would jeopardize my own inheritance. Redeem it for yourself; you may have my right of redemption, for I cannot redeem it" (4:6).[9] Here was his answer: The *land*—yes! The *wife and the kinsman responsibilities*—no! He could not claim the land and refuse to marry Ruth, and he knew it, so he backed out on both.

Whatever the reason, the nearer kinsman saw the responsibility of marrying Ruth as a burden. Boaz saw the responsibility as a blessing. Isn't it interesting how two people can look at the same thing with such different eyes? Boaz saw Ruth as a woman of great worth, and the responsibility of carrying on his kinsman's name as a worthwhile and godly endeavor. He appreciated the value of what he had been offered and demonstrated his eagerness and willingness to take the role of kinsman redeemer. In holding back, the nearer kinsman lost out. His name is never told to us. I find that interesting. His main interest was preserving his inheritance and his name and, ironically, his name isn't even mentioned in the book.

Nobody remembers.

Nobody cares.

All his life, Boaz had been training for this one momentous choice, though he didn't know it. But in that moment, he made a choice based on the character and godliness he had cultivated. For him the choice was easy. Cultivating the character and godliness to make the right choice had been much harder.

Boaz chose wisely.

Therefore, Boaz was blessed.

WHAT ARE YOU REHEARSING FOR?

Emblazoned on Boaz's spiritual coat of arms were kindness, righteousness, and selflessness. He practiced these characteristics until they became natural for him. What's being forged on your spiritual coat of arms? What decisive, critical moment in your life will reveal you as authentic? What are you rehearsing for?

Kindness or apathy?

Righteousness or compromise?

Selflessness or selfishness?

We are all being prepared for great moments in our lives. Oh, they may not be great in the eyes of history, or current events, and no one may write a book on them, but they will be great to us, because they will be epochs and turning points in our lives. You have already experienced some of these great moments and decisions. They had a big impact on your life, for good or for bad. The important question, however, is whether you're ready for the next one.

When that next moment comes, *and it will come*, will your character reveal itself as authentic? Will you be proud of your actions? You are rehearsing right now for that moment! Your past decisions may not have been ones that made you proud, and your present character may make you ashamed, but the wonderful thing about being a Christian is that nothing is irreversible. Yesterday is history—it's gone. An inauthentic character can be changed; your response in great moments can be changed. You can be known for something other than failure.

But the change has to begin now, today—a commitment to begin cultivating godly characteristics in your life. Might I suggest at least three?

Kindness.

Righteousness.

Selflessness.

CHAPTER 8

Naomi's Restoration

*Springtime . . . invites you to try out its splendor
. . . to believe anew. To realize that the same Lord
who renews the trees with buds and blossoms is
ready to renew your life with hope and courage.*

Charles R. Swindoll

ONE DAY, IN THE NEIGHBORHOOD MY WIFE, Annette, grew up in, her neighbor drove up to his house in his pickup truck pulling a trailer. On this trailer was a rusted-out shell of a car—in fact, a rusted chassis and engine were all that identified it as an automobile. It had no doors or windows. The strange part to Annette was that her neighbor Ken, who brought it home, was so excited about it. The stranger part was that he had paid five thousand dollars for this piece of junk. The neighbors probably thought he was crazy.

Undaunted, Ken began work on it, often late into the night and on weekends. He rebuilt the car from the chassis and suspension up. He sandblasted the body and rebuilt the engine. What original parts he could buy, he bought; parts he couldn't find, he made. He was by trade a tool and die maker. He made new pistons, rings, rods, and other parts he needed. He had the windshield and windows specially made. Springs in the seat cushions had to be designed and made.

For the upholstery, he sent away to South America to get high-quality leather. There is no barbed wire in South America to scar up the cattle's hide, thus insuring that he could get unblemished leather. You see, Ken knew the value of that rusted-out car he had bought for five thousand dollars. This was the third time he had rebuilt a car.

Ken went to car shows and bought original speedometers and gauges. He painted the car the pale yellow color that it had had on the original showroom floor. When it was finally finished, Annette, who had watched Ken work on the car, got to ride in it along San Clemente's main boulevard while onlookers gazed, admired, and pointed.

For those of you who are familiar with car shows and their point system, the finished product was a 98-point car. It was 98 percent original. The car was named after Auburn, Indiana. What Ken had found and restored was a 1929 Auburn Cord.

Restoration!

Restored classic automobiles, especially vintage ones, are among the most sought-after items in our world today. Few people are qualified to truly restore these cars to their original state or better. Few can look at something that has deteriorated, or endured the ravages of time in someone's field or dilapidated garage, and see anything of value. Most people see a hunk of rusted iron, a piece of junk. Ken, looking with the eyes of an expert and classic car enthusiast, saw what others missed. He recognized the value of this piece of car, and he saw its potential with his restoration expertise applied to it.

A number of years ago, Ken sold that five-thousand-dollar hunk of junk for forty-eight thousand dollars at an antique car auction in Santa Barbara. Its value today would be far greater. When Ken finished the restoration, it no longer took an expert to see its value and beauty.

I share this story with you because the last verses of Ruth 4, verses 13–22, end the story of Naomi and Ruth. They conclude God's process of restoration in the life of Naomi, for as we've seen, God is also in the restoration business. Where Ken restored cars, God restores lives. Naomi's life had crashed; it was a wreck. In these last few verses, we see how God had restored that crashed and bent life. But more importantly, as we look at the book and the end product, we see Naomi's restoration in the context of a greater process.

We've looked at specifics of how God restores us when distress hits, how He forces us to reexamine His character when we're in pain, how He transforms our desires, and how we model His character until it becomes natural to us, giving us authentic character that withstands testing and blesses us. Now we look at the bigger picture: God as our redeemer, restorer, and sustainer. In verses 14–16, we see the women confirm this to Naomi:

> Then the women said to Naomi, "Blessed is the LORD who has not left you without a redeemer today, and may his name become famous in Israel. May he also be to you a restorer of life and a sustainer of your old age; for your daughter-in-law, who loves you and is better to you than seven sons, has given birth to him." Then Naomi took the child and laid him in her lap, and became his nurse.

When the women told Naomi that the child Obed would be her redeemer and restorer and sustainer, they correctly prefaced that by saying, "Blessed is the LORD who has not left you." They recognized that behind the baby Obed, God had redeemed, restored, and sustained Naomi. God had not left her. Mara would no longer be her name. She was again Naomi, "the pleasant one." Could she have ever imagined this ending to her life?

GOD AS OUR REDEEMER

Let's return to the first part of verse 14: "Then the women said to Naomi, 'Blessed is the LORD who has not left you without a *redeemer* today'" (emphasis added).

The dictionary tells us that the word *redeem* has several meanings:

1. to recover (property) by discharging an obligation
2. to ransom, free, or rescue by paying a price
3. to free from the consequences of sin
4. to remove the obligation by payment
5. to make good (a promise) by performing
6. to atone for[1]

Verse 14 says that God had redeemed Naomi. Naomi knew God as her redeemer, the Old Testament spoke of God as her redeemer, and I believe Naomi had a tight grip on that truth.[2] Nowhere in the book of Ruth does it appear that she ever struggled with this fact, and her comments throughout the book seem to reinforce her faith in God, even in the midst of her disillusionment with Him for allowing her life to be so painful. Those of us who have placed our faith in Jesus know that He bought and redeemed us by His sacrificial death on the cross, and like Naomi, we usually don't struggle with this truth. What we struggle with is God's character when our life crashes. Our poor decisions and the consequences of our sins require a heavenly Redeemer to free us and help us to recover what our sin has cost us.

Naomi's life had degenerated to the point that she was spiritually rusting away as a destitute widow in Israel. What Naomi might have overlooked is a truth that I often overlook, and that is that God's redeeming ministry is never over in my life. While I never again need deliverance from hell or to be forgiven for all of my sins (I am forever delivered from that by Christ's work), yet I am continually in need of deliverance from some poor decision or new accident of life. I keep colliding with life and its problems and getting dented, bent, and seemingly put out of commission. Sometimes I feel like I'm in the same condition as that old rusting hunk of a car.

It is then that God reminds me that His redeeming ministry, His ministry of delivering me from life's distresses, is past, present, and future. As David faced the prospect of his life hitting rock bottom when Absalom his son took over his kingdom and sought to kill him, he wrote these words: "Surely goodness and lovingkindness will follow me all the day of my life, and I will dwell in the house of the LORD forever" (Psalm 23:6). David knew that God was his deliverer. God's character insured that good things would follow David all his life—even a life that had its share of pain, failure, and disappointment, as David's did. The same God who had delivered David from Goliath and the Philistines would deliver him from this danger as well. David knew well the character of his God.

Face it—we still need rescue from the disasters and distress of life. The cornerstone of my faith is that God never goes out of the salvage business. God doesn't have a junkyard where He places Christians who have experienced great failure or pain, even if the failure was our fault. He doesn't take us out of circulation, He just begins the process of restoring us—repairing our broken lives and putting us back into service.

In the first chapter of Ruth, through no fault of her own, Naomi's life had crashed, and she needed someone to pick up the pieces and restore her. God knew what Naomi needed most. He didn't send her a book, a tract, a CD, or a get-well card. He sent her a redeemer, in the form of a baby, and this wouldn't be the last redeemer who would come in the form of a baby: "Therefore the Lord Himself will give you a sign: Behold, a virgin will be with child and bear a son, and she will call His name Immanuel" (Isaiah 7:14).

Naomi's baby, Ruth's son Obed, would grow up and, in Naomi's extreme old age, provide for her financially and carry on her husband's name in Israel. It was Obed's responsibility to do so. That baby would provide the emotional outlet for loving that she so desperately needed. That baby would reaffirm to others God's hand in her life. That baby would confirm to her once and for all that God loves her. She could truthfully say, "God loves me! He really does! He never stopped. He cared enough for me to want to restore my life, joy, and hope."

God redeems because it is His nature to do so. He is the God of mercy and loving-kindness. This is true not because He was merciful and loving in a few great moments in the past, but because that is how God acts, always and forever. Were it not for His mercy, none of us would have any hope. Because of His mercy, we can all have hope.

Restoration involves being able to find value in something that others don't or can't, and being willing to invest in something, redeeming it, so that the process of restoration can be carried on. Once when I was trying to explain to a group of seventh and eighth graders how much God loves us, I took out my wallet and withdrew a crisp five-dollar bill. I waved it around and asked if anyone wanted it. Every hand shot up! Then I crumpled it in a ball and threw it on the ground. I asked if anyone still wanted it. Every hand shot up again! Then I stepped on it with my shoes. Did anyone still want it? I asked. Again, every hand shot up. You see, no matter how crumpled or dirty that five-dollar bill became, its value never changed. The bill was worth five dollars dirty or clean. So it is with us. Though our lives can become crumpled, stepped on, and otherwise degraded, our value to Him never changes, which is why He seeks to restore us.

GOD AS OUR RESTORER

When I was working my way through college and seminary, I made a living hanging wallpaper, so I needed a truck. I bought—or redeemed (*rescued*, really)—a 1955 Chevy half-ton pickup. A classic! The body was in pretty good condition, and I thought it would be fun to restore it. I bought it for $900. Upon reflection, I paid about $890 more than it was worth, but as they say, beauty is in the eye of the beholder (or sucker).

The problem with my plan to restore the truck was that I had neither the money nor the know-how to accomplish this formidable feat. I had spent all my money buying this "primer gray beauty," and one month later, when the engine died, I had to borrow money to get a new engine. As for the technical part of the problem, the actual mechanical know-how necessary to restore a machine, I had less of that than money. My mechanical know-how has always run in the deficit. I've owned a Honda Pilot for seven years, and I still haven't completely figured out how the stereo system works. Buying the truck was one of those "it seemed like a good idea at the time" moments.

To display my mechanical prowess, I needed the man I bought the truck from to show me how to unlatch the hood—I couldn't figure it out. What was wrong with this picture? You see, while I had lots of desire and zeal (those have always been my strong points), I lacked the resources and know-how to complete the project of restoring that old '55 pickup.

That's why these last few verses in Ruth, especially verse 15, are so special to me. They reinforce the truth that God knows how to restore lives that have crashed. "May he also be to you a restorer of life and a sustainer of your old age; for your daughter-in-law, who loves you and is better to you than seven sons, has given birth to him" (Ruth 4:15). God restored Naomi's life through a baby, baby

Obed, born to a daughter-in-law who she didn't even mention to the women of her town when she arrived back in Israel, but who would later take her place in the daughter-in-law hall of fame.

This proves to me that God alone knows how to restore lives. He alone truly understands what it takes to fulfill my life. He alone has the resources and the know-how to restore my life when it has crashed. It's so tragic to me when I see people flock to self-help seminars about how to restore your life, give your life meaning, repair your broken heart, and help you "take charge" of your life! The assumption is that the speakers from out of town with the briefcases are actually fulfilled themselves, like movie stars who we assume are completely happy. This is a mirage. They aren't in control of their lives, no matter what they say.

Anyone who tries to restore his or her life apart from the truths found in the word of God is never going to be able to fix it right, because we do not properly understand its design. People are good at fixing machines or cars or furniture because we designed them. We struggle with fixing lives because we didn't design them. Where do you get the parts to restore a life? Who, besides God, really knows what our lives were designed to be? Who, besides God, knows what would bring us ultimate fulfillment, purpose, and joy? Who, besides God, knows all the places we're broken and how to restore us to our original condition?

God knew exactly what it would take to restore Naomi's life: a Moabite named Ruth, a second-string kinsman redeemer named Boaz, and a divine gift named Obed. (*Obed* means "servant"; his name suggests his ministry to Naomi.) Do you think anyone on the face of the earth could have engineered that restoration job? Naomi started off with a husband and two sons, and then she lost them all. But God, the great restorer, knew how to put her life back together. He restored joy and fulfillment to her life, something she probably never thought could happen again.

When my car breaks down, I seek qualified professionals to restore it to its original condition. When distress hits and my life crashes, I seek God. To do less is foolishness.

GOD AS OUR SUSTAINER

The Hebrew word translated "sustaining" refers to someone providing the necessities of life when you are unable to provide for yourself.

After a car has been bought and lovingly restored, it needs to be cared for, or it will cease to stay restored for very long. Weather, time, and use have a deteriorating effect on a car. The sun oxidizes the paint. The wear of sitting and riding in it eventually tears and unravels the upholstery. Asphalt and the weight of the car eventually wear down the rubber tires. The internal friction and heat of the engine eventually cause parts to wear down.

Life has a deteriorating effect on us as well. The elements of life wear us down, even if our lives have been restored. Problems don't vanish from our lives, and we aren't insulated from distress. God never restores us in order to place us in a protected showroom somewhere. He wants us to drive around town as advertisements to our neighbors of the kind of restoration He does.

Naomi, apart from God's work in her life, had no hope. She had been left a destitute widow. Alone, she might have been able to sustain herself physically, although it would have been difficult. But we are not just biological animals. We also have a spirit that can be crushed and emotions that can be overwhelmed if we get too discouraged. What Naomi needed as much as food and shelter, maybe even more so, was love, security, and most of all . . . hope.

It is amazing to see how God designed these very provisions into Naomi's restoration. In Ruth and Boaz, she had love and security. In baby Obed, she had love, security, and hope. In her eyes, hope was spelled b-a-b-y b-o-y! Obed would not just help to sustain her physically as he grew up and assumed that responsibility, he would help to fill a hole that was left by the death of her husband and two sons. That was essential to sustaining Naomi, and God alone truly knew that. Her husband and her son's names would not die out; Obed would carry them on. She might even live long enough to see Obed's son! That's hope! Verse 16 shows how closely she was able to bond with Obed: "Then Naomi took the child and laid him in her lap, and became his nurse." She became a live-in nanny grandmother. I personally believe being a live-in nanny grandmother is the secret dream of a lot of grandmas I have met. You have to see how wonderful this is: God doesn't just restore her, He sustains her. He provides for her continuing needs.

God loves Naomi just as much as He ever did. It wasn't because He didn't love Naomi that He took her husband and sons. We can't always know the *why* of God's will—but we can trust His character and love for us, displayed forever on the cross. His love for us is everlasting. Naomi just needed a visible and tangible reminder of His love.

Before I leave this, let me call your attention to the last part of verse 15: "May he also be to you a restorer of life and a sustainer of your old age; for your daughter-in-law, who loves you and is better to you than seven sons, has given birth to him." Seven sons was the picture of the perfect Hebrew family, the supreme blessing that could come to a family. The women looked at Ruth and told Naomi, "Ruth is of more value to you than seven sons. You've got the better-than-ideal family situation."

Does God know how to sustain, or doesn't He?

THE PRICE OF RESTORATION

The story of Ruth and Naomi was truly one of being lovingly restored by God. When God finished restoring Naomi, she had gone from rust and breakdown to better than original condition. God is the great redeemer, restorer, and sustainer of life! We need to be constantly aware that God redeems, restores, and sustains our lives continually.

God is still in the restoration business. If you are a Christian, you need to know that God is lovingly restoring you, even if right now you feel like Naomi did when her life crashed. Be assured that the great designer of life doesn't make mistakes. He is doing what is necessary to restore your life.

God made us in His image, therefore we are worth restoring. God knows our original condition, and no matter how bad our life has crashed, He sees the potential, the value of restoring it. He knows it's not a waste. God declared our value to Him when He sent His precious, beloved Son to pay the price necessary to buy us out of slavery to sin and hell. C. S. Lewis once said, "It costs God nothing, so far as we know, to create nice things: but to convert rebellious wills cost His crucifixion."[3] The price of our restoration from death into life was eternally high, a price unreachable to us. Yet His restoration of us involves not simply a onetime event (at salvation), but a continued process where He uses all of life and its experiences—including distress—to restore what life on earth and sin can damage.

To restore is not always to replace with the same—at times, that's just not possible. To restore is "to put or bring back into existence or use; to put again in possession of something."[4] That's precisely what He did with Naomi and with Ruth.

You're next.

Discussion Questions

CHAPTER 1: RUTH'S GODLY CHARACTER

1. Place a check mark next to the most accurate description of your spiritual heritage:
   - ❏ Strongly Christian
   - ❏ Mildly Christian
   - ❏ Mildly religious
   - ❏ Agnostic (doubt)
   - ❏ Atheist (disbelief)
   - ❏ Apathetic

   Has your spiritual heritage helped you spiritually or hindered you? Why?

2. Naomi introduced Ruth to the God of Israel. Did you have a "Naomi" in your life who pointed you to God? What made that person so effective?

3. Recall the line, "Some things in our lives require removal to guarantee our continued growth." What has God removed from your life that resulted in your faith growing?

4. Can you think of an area in your life where you believe God wants to bring change—but you are resisting it? What is your greatest fear?

5. Over time, our choices eventually become our habits. We

begin to respond to situations in the same way. Think of two to three good responses or habits that you have developed when faced with difficulties, and two to three bad habits you have developed. What can you learn about yourself through this exercise?

6. Has God ever led you into the unknown? What lessons did you learn about Him and about yourself through following Him?

7. Name the people you know whom God has so transformed that you would call them godly. What qualities do you most admire in them? (If possible, talk to your "godly" people and ask them what God did to change them.)

8. All of us trust in something. Next to the three options below, place a percentage of how much of your trust is in that area, with the total adding up to 100 percent (e.g., God 30%, My resources 35%, My abilities 35%).

    *   God _____%
    *   My resources _____%
    *   My abilities _____%

    Where do you place your trust?

9. Can you think of someone who showed you "kindness in a lonely place," as Ruth showed Naomi? What did he or she do?

10. Think of several ways in which you are different from others and the experiences that have helped to make you different. This could include your passions, talents, interests, etc. Have you considered that God made you different *for His purposes*? Does that thought encourage or discourage you, and why?

APPLICATION: God wants to make you a person of excellence first in His eyes, and then in the eyes of others. As you look honestly at your own life, what three areas do you think God most wants to restore in you? Write down your answer.

ACTION: As you go through this study, keep the list of three things you think God wants to restore in your life handy. Ask Him to help you release these things to Him, to stop resisting the necessary change. Feel free to revise the list as you learn more about yourself and God's Word.

CHAPTER 2: NAOMI'S CHARACTER BLEMISHES

1. "Sometimes our own sinfulness and mistakes create the distress in our lives, but not always! Some distress we encounter, the pain we experience, is not related to any sin on our part, but is God's way of adding depth and maturity to our lives." Do you agree or disagree with this statement? Why?

2. Give an example of when your sin caused you distress, and another of when you think your distress was not caused by your failure. Do you feel different about the two types of distress? If so, why?

3. Ruth was clearly Naomi's closest companion in distress. Who is your closest companion in your distress? What makes that person different from everyone else?

4. When others try to minister to you in your distress, how do you initially respond to them?

5. Finish this thought: The greatest struggle for me in letting people minister to me in my distress is . . .

6. God asks the question, "Can you trust me now?" What do you think is the area He is asking you to trust Him in?

7. The Scriptures tell us that God has a unique purpose in our distress. Think of one distress in which you can clearly see God's purpose for your life—and another where the purpose is not clear to you yet.

8. Our purpose in creation is to glorify God. Think about how God can be glorified in your response to Him in your greatest distress. Is your present response to distress glorifying Him? In what way? If not, what changes do you feel God would have you make in your heart and actions?

APPLICATION: In the process of restoring your life, God wants to help you gain perspective on your distress and gain from it what He intended. You may have been resisting the idea that your distress could have value in His eyes. Will you allow God to meet you at a deeper level than ever before in your distress? Write a short letter of permission to God to use your distress to grow you spiritually. Be honest. Be real. Express your hopes, fears, and desires to Him who loves you.

ACTION: Carefully consider those people who have either ministered to you in your distress or attempted to minister to you. Write them each a note of appreciation and thanks (or an apology if you rebuffed their attempts). Remind them that you are a work in progress, but that you thank God for them and their concern for you.

CHAPTER 3: ELIMILECH'S BAD DECISION

1. Elimelech fell for the myth of the greener grass—the idea that he could find safety and security and success outside of

God's plan and will. Can you think of a time when you fell for this myth? What were the results?

2. Can you name at least two promises of God that you have seen Him honor in your life?

3. What promises of God are you still waiting on Him to fulfill?

4. What is the one thing that you want "fixed" now? In what way are you tempted to try and "fix" the problem outside of His will?

5. The search for security apart from God is a temptation for us all. Why do you think it's easier to place your trust in yourself or others rather than in God?

6. Can you think of a time when someone else's decision to take a shortcut affected you negatively?

7. In those moments of weakness when you chose to circumvent the promises of God, what messages were your actions saying about your belief and trust in God?

APPLICATION: This is an important time for you to ask yourself sincerely what you really believe about God—not just what you say you believe. Take some time to think and write down what you believe about God. Only list those things you absolutely believe about God.

ACTION: Now it's time to get honest with God. Admit to God that you struggle to believe that He will honor His promises in your life. Admit the weakness of your faith. Then, ask Him to strengthen your faith in the areas you feel weakest in. Make these areas a matter of regular prayer. To strengthen your faith is a prayer that is completely within His will—so you don't have to wonder whether He wants to answer in a positive way. He wants to restore not only your life, but your confidence in Him and His promises.

CHAPTER 4: RUTH'S GODLY EXAMPLE

1. God has specialty people for each one of us—people who compliment our strengths and challenge our weaknesses. Can you name three or four people whom God used to strengthen and encourage you? In what areas did each person strengthen you?

2. Our specialty people challenge us to nobler ambitions, as Ruth challenged Naomi. What noble ambitions have some of your specialty people challenged you to?

3. Can you think of a time when someone who cared about you challenged you to nobler ambitions and you didn't respond well? Why was it hard for you to respond to their challenge?

4. In the past, how have you made it difficult for your specialty people to help you? Did you consider at the time that God might use these people to challenge and encourage you to better things, or did you see their offer of help as merely meddling?

5. Can you name one or two people who remained committed to you even when you tried to push them away?

6. Think of several attitudes your specialty people have *modeled* to you that you lack. List them in their order of importance to you.

7. Sometimes pain dulls our perspective. How have your specialty people been able to give you a perspective that you didn't have? What were they able to show you that you couldn't see?

APPLICATION: The Proverbs tell us that "many a man proclaims his own loyalty, but who can find a trustworthy man?" (20:6). This truth acknowledges that specialty people are rare. Have you ever shared with your specialty people how they have positively affected your life and your faith in God? Don't assume your specialty people know how you feel about them, or how much they changed your life. Give them a call, write them a note, or send them a card. The Bible teaches that we are to give honor to whom honor is due.

ACTION: As God has given you specialty people to positively affect your life, He has called you to be a specialty person to someone else. You need to determine to be someone's Ruth, the one who gently challenges another to nobler ambitions, remains committed even when the person makes it difficult, models attitudes that person sorely lacks at the moment, and graciously provides a needed perspective on life and God. Ask God to lead you to the right person that you might be a specialty person to him or her.

CHAPTER 5: NAOMI'S REAPPRAISAL OF GOD'S CHARACTER

1. It is hard to understand the real character of God when we are in pain. In your moments of pain and distress, what part of God's character do you struggle with most?

2. There are times in life when it seems like everything that could go wrong does go wrong. Describe such a time in your life. What did it begin to do to your belief in God's character?

3. List several positive assumptions about God that you began to question when trouble hit. In hindsight, do you think your assumptions were correct, underdeveloped, or wrong?

4. Did your assumptions about God come from God's revelation of himself in the Bible, or from another place? What might the "other place" have been?

5. Have you been tempted to stop believing in God because of pain He has allowed in your life? Are you there now? What do you want God to do for you that He hasn't?

6. When you hear the phrase "God is faithful," what do you assume He is faithful to do for you? Are those assumptions promises He has made?

7. Life is dangerous, with calamities and trials awaiting us all, and we often feel vulnerable as a result. Make a list of what you recall God promises to protect us from and another list of things He *doesn't* promise to protect us from. Compare your lists with other Christians, especially mature believers. What were you expecting to be protected from that God has not promised?

8. In what ways does God's compassion differ from the compassion we show others?

APPLICATION: Try to list at least ten ways that God has been faithful to you, protected you, or shown you compassion. If you have trouble with your list (which can happen when you're in pain), have some mature Christians help you.

ACTION: Take some time to reappraise God's character. Write down what each statement means in your life:

God is faithful.

God protects me.

God loves me.

Look up Scriptures that speak of these characteristics of God. Compare what God says about himself to what you have written.

Ask God to help you to see Him as He really is—ask Him to reveal himself more fully to you. Ask God to restore your confidence in His character.

CHAPTER 6: NAOMI'S TRANSFORMED DESIRES

1. "There are few more painful processes in life than the one in which we are forced to reexamine our dearest desires, and to finally, with great pain and tears of anguish, let them go." What desires have you had to let go in your life?

2. Have you reached a goal, only to find that the process affected you in a negative way? Was the goal worth attaining?

3. Finish this sentence in light of the hopes you have for your life: I wish I had . . .

4. Have you ever tried to define God's work and character by how you felt about Him at a particular moment? What helped you to see God more clearly?

5. What are your unfulfilled desires? Are you frustrated because your deepest and most intense desires aren't being realized? Do you sense God asking you to let any of them go?

6. Have you been tempted to take a shortcut to fulfill your desire? What happened as a result?

7. Have you been blessed in a way you never expected? What were the circumstances?

8. Reflect upon the experience of Lilian Doerksen. How would you rate your life satisfaction so far? Explain your answer.

❑ I've think I've definitely lived a worthwhile
  life.

❑ I think I've lived a mostly worthwhile life.

❑ I hope I've lived a worthwhile life.

❑ I need a "do over" in life.

APPLICATION: Identify several of your deepest desires. If desires are the battleground for our souls, then what side is winning in your life? What desires does God need to transform in you?

ACTION: Take a moment to review some of the major life decisions you've made. What were the desires behind these decisions? Did you run each decision through the following grid: Will it honor God? Will it enhance my spiritual life? Will it enhance my family life? Will it have eternal value?

CHAPTER 7: BOAZ'S AUTHENTIC CHARACTER

1. List three of your heroes. What qualities must a person possess to qualify as your hero?

2. What shows you that a person's character is genuine, not merely a pose?

3. Did you ever have a hero let you down? What disappointed you most about that experience?

4. "Sadly, we don't usually appreciate the wisdom of God when He calls us to practice godly virtues like kindness— not understanding that He frequently chooses to bless our lives through these very characteristics." What blessings do we miss when we choose not to practice kindness?

5. Have you ever been surprised by kindness you received? Why did you consider it unlikely you would receive this kindness?

6. Surely Boaz's and Ruth's kindness had been abused over the years. Has your kindness been abused? If so, how did the abuse affect your determination to be kind?

7. Can you think of an experience or opportunity when you had to choose righteousness (being just and honorable) over unrighteousness? What were you risking by choosing righteousness?

8. What is the most selfless act anyone has ever done for you? What do you think is the most selfless act you have ever done for someone else?

9. "Unless you live extraordinarily behind the scenes, you will never act extraordinarily when you are finally and unexpectedly thrust into the spotlight." Choose one of the options below and explain why you chose it.

   ❑ I'm ready for my spotlight moment.
   ❑ I hope I'm ready for my spotlight moment.
   ❑ I doubt that I'm ready for my spotlight moment.
   ❑ I know I'm not ready for my spotlight moment.

APPLICATION: Spend some time thinking about what your current choices in life have you really rehearsing for. Would you choose kindness, trust, righteousness, or selflessness if the pressure was increased? This involves more self-honesty than we normally allow ourselves. Ask God to help you to see yourself as you really are, not simply as you think you are.

ACTION: When God acts, He acts by virtue of His perfect character. In other words, He doesn't need to choose good over evil, the right thing to do over the shortcut—He always does what is right. We, however, have a choice constantly. Right now you have an opportunity to:

Be kind to someone.

Choose righteousness when choosing the temptation would be easier.

Act selflessly in a matter dear to your heart.

Take time to pray and ask God how this month, this week, even this very day, you can show kindness, righteousness, and selflessness in specific ways with specific people in your life. Make a conscious decision to look for opportunities to do this over and over. It's never too late to start doing the right thing!

CHAPTER 8: NAOMI'S RESTORATION

1. At the beginning of chapter 8, I shared the story of the restored classic car. As you consider where you are at in God's restoration of you, how would you describe yourself? (Examples: a house in need of renovation, an unfinished piece of clothing, a plane in need of wings and a propeller, a wagon in need of wheels, etc.)

2. Since we are unable to completely rescue or redeem ourselves, what is it that God needs to rescue you from?

3. Four definitions of *redeem* are:

   To give back: return

   To put back into use or service again

   To put or bring back into a former or original state

   To put again in possession of something

As you consider your current distress, which of these definitions would you most like to see God do in your life? Why?

4. Since God alone truly knows how to restore a life, have you considered that He might use means that you did not expect to restore you? Are you open to that? Have you already determined what God would need to do to restore your life—thereby setting yourself up for disappointment if He chooses another means?

5. How has God shown us through the Scriptures and through Jesus that He loves us enough to want to restore us?

6. Life has a deteriorating effect on us. What elements of life have begun to wear you down?

7. In what way do you feel you most need to be sustained right now? What is it you need that God has to provide?

APPLICATION: The closer we grow to our Lord, the greater is our joy and blessing. Before our lives can be restored, our relationship with Him needs to be restored. Spend time praying and seeking God. Tell Him how you want your heart, and your attitude toward Him, restored. Admit your inability to restore yourself.

ACTION: To allow God to work in our distress and brokenness, we need to admit that God made us, and only He knows what would bring about our restoration. Write a letter to God, allowing Him to do whatever He needs to do to restore your life. Don't write this letter until you can mean it. The letter doesn't have to be long, just honest. When you are growing weak and feel tempted to fall back into previous patterns of distrust and "fixing it yourself," bring out this letter and recommit to your decision to have God restore your life.

Notes

INTRODUCTION: IS THIS YOUR STORY?

1. *Merriam-Webster Online*, 11th ed., "distress," accessed September 13, 2010, http://www.merriam-webster.com/dictionary/distress; *Merriam-Webster Online*, 11th ed., s.v. "restore," accessed September 13, 2010, http://www.merriam-webster.com/dictionary/restore.

CHAPTER 1: RUTH'S GODLY CHARACTER

1. Chemosh was the god of the Moabites and possibly the Ammonites (Numbers 21:29; 1 Kings 11:7). In 2 Kings 3:27 we read of a defeated king of Moab sacrificing his oldest son as a burnt offering to Chemosh in payment or appeasement after their loss in battle to Israel.
2. Ruth is one of only four women listed in the lineage of our Lord. Ruth and her husband Boaz had a son named Obed, Obed was the father of Jesse, and Jesse was the father of David.
3. J. Sidlow Baxter, *Baxter's Explore the Book* (Grand Rapids: Zondervan, 1987), 27.

CHAPTER 2: NAOMI'S CHARACTER BLEMISHES

1. Norman Cousins, *Draper's Book of Quotations for the Christian World*, ed. Edythe Draper (Wheaton, IL: Tyndale, 1992), #2254.

2. The Associated Press, "Renaissance Treasure Found in Pennsylvania," November 24, 1999.

3. Bob Kilpatrick, "(In My Life) Lord, Be Glorified," © 1978 Bob Kilpatrick Ministries.

4. A. B. Simpson, *A Larger Christian Life* (Christian Alliance Publishing Co., 1890), 111.

CHAPTER 3: ELIMELECH'S BAD DECISION

1. Baal's female counterpart was Ashtoreth. Sexual intercourse between these two gods was believed to regulate the fertility of the earth and its creatures.

2. Arthur E. Cundall and Leon Morris, *Judges & Ruth*, Tyndale Old Testament Commentaries (Downers Grove, IL: InterVarsity Press, 1968), 249.

3. James S. Hewitt, ed., *Illustrations Unlimited* (Wheaton, IL: Tyndale, 1988), 247.

4. D. L. Moody, "Colorful Sayings from Colorful Moody," compiled by Mary Ann Jeffreys, *Christian History and Biography*, January 1, 1990, http://www.ctlibrary.com/ch/1990/issue25/2508.html.

5. C. S. Lewis, *Mere Christianity* (San Francisco: HarperSan-Francisco, 2001), 132.

6. See Genesis 35:19, 48:7; Ruth 4:11; Micah 5:2. We have no way of knowing why the city's name changed. The use of the old name for Bethlehem points to the idea that Elimelech's family was old and established.

7. While Deuteronomy 23:3–4 states that Moabites weren't to be admitted to the congregation of Israel, neither their offspring, the law did not prohibit marriage with a Moabite. Deuteronomy 7:3 refers only to Canaanites and other dwellers in the land. (Cundall and Morris, *Judges & Ruth*, 250.)

8. "Find Us Faithful." Words and music by Jon Mohr. Copyright © 1987 Jonathan Mark Music, Birdwing Music. All rights reserved. Used by permission.

9. R. C. Sproul, *Objections Answered* (Ventura, CA: Regal, 1978), 84.

10. Hewett, *Illustrations Unlimited*, 56–57.

CHAPTER 4: RUTH'S GODLY EXAMPLE

1. Eberhard Bodenschatz, "Temperature, Wind Account for Snowflake's Unique Shape," Cornell Center for Materials Research, February 11, 1999, http://www.ccmr.cornell.edu/education/ask/index.html?quid=177.

2. Albert Barnes, *Barnes' Notes on the Old and New Testaments* (Grand Rapids: Baker, 1996), 473.

3. J. Sidlow Baxter, "The Book of Ruth," *Explore the Book* (Grand Rapids: Zondervan, 1966), 36.

4. John Zant, "Digging Deep: Olympic athletes focus on the positives as they go for the gold," *The Independent*, August 14, 2008, 49.

CHAPTER 5: NAOMI'S REAPPRAISAL OF GOD'S CHARACTER

1. Lyle W. Dorsett, "Helen Joy Davidman (Mrs. C. S. Lewis) 1915–1960: A Portrait," *C. S. Lewis Institute*, http://www.cslewisinstitute.org/cslewis/JDavidmanProfile.htm.

2. C. S. Lewis, *A Grief Observed*, (San Francisco: HarperSan-Francisco, 1996), 6–7.

3. Henry Ward Beecher, *Draper's Book of Quotations*, #4641.

4. Hannah Hurnard, *Draper's Book of Quotations*, #968.

5. Chuck Swindoll, *Quest for Character* (Grand Rapids: Zondervan, 1993), 18–19.

6. From Haddon Robinson, "How Does God Keep His Promises?" *Preaching Today*, audiocassette no. 130, available online at http://www.preachingtodaysermons.com/rohahowdogod.html.

7. Ibid.

8. A number of commentators describe Ruth as a beautiful young maiden. Now, I may need to apologize someday in heaven, but nowhere in the book of Ruth does it say that she is. In fact, to say she was physically beautiful does her a disservice. Physical beauty does not need to be present to finish the mental picture of attractive and desirable. The fact that Boaz shows Ruth special attention almost immediately may be what led some commentators to believe she was beautiful. But as we look at the whole story, we see that it was Ruth's *actions* that initially caught Boaz's attention, not her physical charms. Ruth's attractiveness to Boaz was prompted by her faithful and selfless love toward Naomi and God. Scripture usually tells us when a person is uncommonly physically attractive (e.g., Esther was chosen to be queen of Babylon for her beauty, Joseph was called handsome, David was called ruddy and handsome). This wasn't the case with Ruth; her real beauty was internal. Further, she didn't have the means to make herself look beautiful because she had become destitute to follow God and Naomi into Israel. She couldn't afford the luxuries of fine clothes, perfumes, and jewelry. Something far more than physical beauty is here, and to hint that her beauty drew Boaz's attention would cheapen her character as well as Boaz's.

9. Philip Yancey, *Disappointment with God* (Grand Rapids: Zondervan, 1997), 203.

10. Ibid., 204.

11. Quoted in ibid., 205–6.

12. Sheldon Vanauken, *A Severe Mercy* (New York: Harper & Row, 1977), 190. Cited in Mark Littleton, *The Storm Within* (Wheaton, IL: Tyndale, 1994), 62–63.

CHAPTER 6: NAOMI'S TRANSFORMED DESIRES

1. Gordon MacDonald, *Living at High Noon* (Old Tappen, NJ: Fleming H. Revell, 1985), 126–27.
2. "Jessica: A New Life," *Playboy*, September 1988, 162. Quoted from Mary Zeiss Stange, "Jessica Hahn's Strange Odyssey from PTL to *Playboy*," *Journal of Feminist Studies in Religion* 6, no. 1 (Spring 1990): 105–16.
3. C. S. Lewis, *A Grief Observed* (New York: HarperCollins, 2001), 37–38.
4. "Biolans Up Close," *Biola Magazine* (Spring 2003), 25.

CHAPTER 7: BOAZ'S AUTHENTIC CHARACTER

1. You can read the entire speech at http://www.historyplace.com/speeches/washington.htm.
2. A contemporary of Washington, Napoleon Bonaparte of France championed the fledgling French Republic and later betrayed it, seizing power and naming himself emperor for life. After defeat in battle at Waterloo and exile, he lamented his country's opinion of him: "They wanted me to be another Washington."
3. C. S. Lewis, *Mere Christianity*, in *The Complete C. S. Lewis Signature Classics* (San Francisco: HarperOne, 2002), 81.
4. Henry Drummond, *Draper's Book of Quotations*, #665.
5. *The Merriam-Webster Dictionary* (software, version 2.6), 2001, s.v. "righteousness."
6. Even today throwing your robe, or blanket, over your bride is a wedding custom in some parts of the East.

7. John Powell, *Draper's Book of Quotations*, #10062.

8. The land could never be ultimately sold, because the law of God stated that in the year of Jubilee, which occurred every fifty years, all land returned to its rightful owner (see Leviticus 25:1–17). Israelites could, however, buy land temporarily and gain its revenue. Since there weren't many opportunities like this, the option was an attractive one to a man who wanted to make money. But only a kinsman redeemer could help you, and only if he was willing.

9. Commentators have suggested reasons why the nearer kinsman might have refused to marry Ruth. Some think he was too poor to sustain the land and a wife, though this seems unlikely, since the land should have brought in more than enough to sustain another mouth or two. Some have suggested that he was superstitious, afraid that marrying a Moabitess might lead to the fate of Mahlon, Ruth's first husband. I lean toward the idea that he thought his son by Ruth might try to lay claim to his present estate as well as the land he would rightfully inherit. The nearer kinsman might not have had a son of his own yet, and he might have been worried about a struggle for his own estate later on, thus jeopardizing his own name.

CHAPTER 8: NAOMI'S RESTORATION

1. *The Merriam-Webster Dictionary* (software, version 2.6), 2001, s.v. "redeem."

2. God is spoken of as the redeemer of His people in many Old Testament verses, including Psalms 19:14 and 78:35; and Isaiah 41:14 and 43:14.

3. C. S. Lewis, *Mere Christianity* (San Francisco: HarperSan-Francisco, 2001), 212.

4. *Merriam-Webster Online*, 11th ed., s.v. "restore," accessed September 10, 2010, http://www.merriam-webster.com/dictionary/restore.

Note to the Reader

The publisher invites you to share your response to the message of this book by writing Discovery House Publishers, P.O. Box 3566, Grand Rapids, MI 49501, USA. For information about other Discovery House books, music, DVDs, or videos, contact us at the same address or call 1-800-653-8333. Find us on the Internet at http://www.dhp.org/ or send e-mail to books@dhp.org.